The
PRIESTHOOD
of the
FAITHFUL

THE
PRIESTHOOD
OF THE
FAITHFUL

by
EMILE-JOSEPH DE SMEDT
Bishop of Bruges, Belgium

JOSEPH M. F. MARIQUE, S.J.

DEUS BOOKS
PAULIST PRESS
(Paulist Fathers)
New York, N. Y.

*Pastoral Letter
Addressed to
Priests, Religious and Lay Apostles
of the
Diocese of Bruges*

A Deus Books Edition of the Paulist Press, 1962, by special arrangement with Desclée De Brower & Cie, Bruges, Belgium

English Translation © 1962 by
The Missionary Society of St. Paul the Apostle
in the State of New York

Library of Congress Catalog Card Number:
62-11628

Manufactured in the United States of America by
Paulist Press, New York, N. Y.

Affectionately Dedicated to His Eminence Cardinal J. E. van Roey on the 35th Anniversary of His Episcopal Consecration.

Contents

7

8 *Contents*

Part Two

THE PEOPLE OF GOD AND THEIR PASTORS

Foreword

The relations between the hierarchy and the faithful is a problem that has been studied and discussed considerably in recent times.[1] What has been accomplished to date? The true mission of the faithful in the Church has long been ignored. Recent popes have repeatedly struggled with this shortcoming,[2] with the result that greater understanding now exists in regard to this matter. The role of the Christian People has been seriously re-evaluated. On the practical side, the lay apostolate has gathered considerable and promising impetus. But in regard to the principles involved, not everything has been cleared up. From the Christian point of view, what then are the roles of clergy and faithful in the Kingdom of God?

Naturally, this subject will never be exhausted. We are dealing here with one of the basic aspects of the life of the Church—one of those mysteries, an exciting reality, whose grandeur human reason here on earth cannot grasp. However, we are not altogether without light on the subject. To a certain degree, faith can dispel the shadows in the mysteries. If our faith is such that it courageously seeks the truth, we shall have a new, broader, and more complete understanding of the People of God.

The Church, that is, faithful and pastors, is nothing else but the continuation on earth of the glorious Christ. The Church is the visible sign of the grace of redemption. Now it is this totality, the People of God led by their priestly hierarchy, which together form "a standard over the nations." [3] This is the "mystery which has been hidden from eternity . . ." [4] whose profound nature the Holy Spirit would have us understand. Let us ask Him, therefore, what relations should prevail between the members of this People.

Many Catholics have not yet sufficiently realized that the apostolate is the business of the whole Church. Theoretically, they are perhaps aware that the hierarchy is not the only active force among the People of God, but in practice, they do not fully understand the basic part that Christ assigns to the Christian People themselves. This erroneous conception is more widespread than one cares to think. It may be found in traditionally Catholic regions, and we see it raising its head in areas newly opened to Christianity. The charge is also made by our separated brethren. In their view, the Catholic Church has under-estimated the responsibilities that properly be-long to laymen. According to them, the Peo-ple of God have only a passive and receptive mission in Catholic doctrine, and their true role is misunderstood or neglected.

Needless to say, all this is not in accord with true Catholic thought. However, we must admit that in practice, the attitude of a con-siderable number of priests and laymen could be classified under the same form of misunder-standing. Fortunately a reaction has set in. Numerous documents emanating from the teaching authority of the Church and many recent publications have emphasized the true doctrine concerning the Christian laity.[5] Fur-thermore, events have shown that the Church places great store on the part the faithful are called to play.[6]

In our own diocese, we are not strangers to one another. Working together for Christ is a habit with us. At regular intervals we meet for liturgical prayer and in the various fields of the apostolate. The success of campaigns undertaken in common have proven that your bishop was right in placing firm confidence in your ability, your zeal, and your apostolic charity. On the other hand, the apostolic work accomplished in your parishes, in your neighborhoods, and in your places of work, bears living witness to the mutual understanding that prevails among us.

Your conduct is that of true apostles of Christ. And we have spoken to you frequently and with frankness about the nature and the requirements of your Christian apostolate.[7] You have listened to our counsels and you have put them into practice with an awareness of present needs. That is why we are now encouraged to give you more substantial food for thought.

In this Pastoral letter which comes to you as the Second Vatican Ecumenical Council is about to open, we intend to speak to you of the royal priesthood of the faithful. We are convinced that a deeper understanding of the priestly character of the People of God will be a powerful contribution to that increase of genuine Christian living in conformity with the gospel, which His Holiness Pope John XXIII expects as a result of the Council. In the words of the Sovereign Pontiff, this will enable the Catholic Church to say to our separated brethren: "This is the Church of Christ. We have endeavored to be true to her, and we have asked the Lord that she may always remain such as He wished her to be."[8]

We humbly pray the Lord Jesus to bless these pages, written out of love for Him and His Church, that they may be an effective call to union in our faith, in charity, and in our apostolate. May they contribute somewhat to intensify the harmony and disinterested collaboration of all those who have received from the Master the signal grace as well as the very serious responsibility of belonging to the royal priesthood of the People of God.

Part One

THE ROYAL

PRIESTHOOD

OF ALL THE FAITHFUL

I
Nature of the Priesthood of All the Faithful

All the faithful are priests. Their priesthood is different from the priesthood conferred by the sacrament of Orders, but the difference is a partial one. It is true that the faithful as such have not officially received the mandate to be the Church's representative before God, and God's representative to the Church. Nevertheless, they share an essential element of all priesthood with ministering priests: a certain power to make an offering in, through, and with Christ. Today Jesus still lives in the midst of His People. By intimate union with Him, the faithful, through Him and in Him, offer their interior life, their praises, their sacrifices, and their apostolic work. Although the priesthood of the faithful is only analogical, it is a genuine priesthood.

While Jesus was fulfilling His priestly, prophetic, and royal mission on earth, He truly lived in the midst of His own People. He did not officiate in a cathedral. He was not a university teacher. He was not seated on a throne. To His first apostles who were to become His intimates, He simply said: "Follow Me." [1] To become a disciple of Christ implied going with Him in the midst of crowds. He trained His disciples then and there through personal experience.

He took them along on His apostolic journeys. Now seated on the slope of a hill, another time in a boat, or sharing His meals with them, He grouped them around Himself and gave them His divine teaching. He shared the life of His People, and He trained those who, while going about their daily tasks, were willing to listen to Him.

It was also in the midst of the Jews and pagans standing around the tribunal of Pontius Pilate, that He made the calm and authoritative affirmation about His royal dignity: "I am a King. This is why I was born, and why I have come into the world, to bear witness to the truth. Everyone who is of the truth hears My voice." [2]

So, too, with His sacrifice. When His hour had come, it was in the open air in the midst of the crowds that He was condemned, martyred, and crucified. On Calvary, surrounded by enemies and a few friends, He, the High Priest, gave His life in sacrifice.

After His resurrection and ascension, Jesus is not separated from His disciples. Christ glorious, Lord of heaven and earth, continues His priesthood in the midst of the chosen People of the New Testament. Much more than this, He bestows His Spirit on His People and makes them share in the priestly mission the Father has entrusted to Him.

Even in the Old Testament Yahweh had chosen Israel to be His chosen People. From the summit of Mt. Sinai He said to Moses: "Therefore, if you hearken to My voice and keep My covenant, you shall be My special possession, dearer to Me than all other people, though all the earth is Mine. You shall be to Me a kingdom of priests, a holy nation." [3]

From that day the Israelites were the People whose mission it was to worship the true God. Of course, there was an hereditary priesthood in the midst of this chosen People charged with ministerial worship. But side by side with this Levitical priesthood was the priesthood of the people themselves; for the whole People was commissioned to recognize Yahweh, to offer Him a sacrifice of praise and honor. And so, alone among all the nations of the world, the People of God constituted, so to speak, a community of priests entrusted with the worship of the King par excellence: *regale sacerdotium, gens sancta* (a holy priesthood, a holy People).

Isaia was speaking of this priesthood when
he saw the dawn of the era of salvation in
which the Messiah and the People redeemed
by Him would add new and higher glory to
the priesthood of the Jewish people: "You
yourselves shall be named priests of the Lord,
ministers of our God you shall be called." [4]

In the New Testament this spiritual priesthood is fully realized in a measure vastly sur-
passing that which preceded it. St. Peter
speaks of it to the first Christians: "Draw near
to Him, a living stone, rejected indeed by men
but chosen and honored by God. Be you yourselves as living stones, built thereon into a
spiritual house, a holy priesthood, to offer
spiritual sacrifices acceptable to God through
Jesus Christ. . . You, however, are a chosen
race, a royal priesthood, a holy nation, a purchased people; that you may proclaim the perfections of Him who has called you out of
darkness into His marvelous light." [5]

When St. Peter ascribes the quality of royal
priesthood to the People of God, is there question of a true priesthood? Are all the faithful
priests? Yes, yours is a real, true, genuine
priesthood. You have what is common to
every priesthood, namely, the capacity to worship God in a manner agreeable to Him. This
disposition is completely realized in Jesus

Christ. Priests of the ministry possess this quality. But when we say that the faithful are themselves priests, it is not merely in the sense of a highly suggestive, though inadequate, resemblance or metaphor. No, we are not merely speaking of a moral obligation by virtue of which the faithful have a personal duty to "offer" to God acts of renunciation and acts of religion. There is more to it than that. All Christians, by virtue of their baptism have received the capacity to make an offering in Christ and with Christ. The Holy Spirit has invested those baptized with a new quality that produces in them the priestly dignity of Jesus Himself in a limited and real, although analogical, sense.

Hence, we can call the People of God a priestly people. The offering they are commissioned to make is a genuine offering,[6] one that the Father recognizes as that for which He sanctified this People. The Christian People, of themselves, do not possess this mission. They received it in Jesus Christ. They possess it by virtue of their dependence on Jesus. The offering of the faithful is agreeable to the Father because Jesus continues to live in His People and has communicated His priestly powers to it.

You are not accustomed to hear yourselves called priests of the Lord. But so it is. To beginners, light food is given. We believe that the time has now come to unfold the dignity that Jesus has conferred on you in all its grandeur. It is true, of course, not all the faithful are part of the ministerial priesthood as priests who have received the sacrament of Holy Orders. Not all have been consecrated to become genuine delegates of their brethren in the faith and the official representatives of Jesus to His People. St. Paul, speaking to the Corinthians, makes a clear-cut distinction: "For we are God's helpers, you are God's tillage, God's building." [7]

Later on, something will be said about the function of the ministerial priesthood among the People of God. The fact remains, no matter what your function in the Church, you participate analogically, to a certain degree, in the priesthood of Jesus, and it is your mission to work with Him. "But to each one of us grace was given according to the measure of Christ's bestowal. . . And He Himself gave some men as apostles, and some as prophets, others again as evangelists, and others as pastors and teachers, in order to perfect the saints for a work of ministry, for building up the body of Christ, until we all attain to the unity of the faith and of the deep knowledge of the Son of God, to perfect manhood, to the mature measure of the fullness of Christ. . . For from Him the whole body (being closely joined and knit together through every joint of the system according to the functioning in due measure of each single part) derives its increase to the building up of itself in love." [8]

It is clear then that we are dealing here with a dignity which is possessed in common by all those who belong to the Mystical Body of Christ. St. Augustine expresses it in a very striking manner: "Just as we call them all *christ* (anointed) because of the mystical chrism (chrisma), so also all are priests by virtue of the fact that they are members of One Priest." [9]

Not only laymen and religious, but ordained priests as well, bishops, even the Pope—all are invested with this basic priesthood. When we come to the eternal kingdom, face to face with God in the beatific vision, when the People of God will have been completely formed, and the ministerial order will have ended its temporary mission, the royal priesthood of the People of God will remain. It will be united for all eternity to the triumphant Jesus, offering to His Father the eternal holocaust of His adoration and gratitude.

II
The
Priestly Work
of the Faithful

The foregoing chapter has indicated the great dignity that Jesus has conferred on all as members of the People of God. Baptism and Confirmation have consecrated and incorporated us in the priestly People of Christ. This is our greatest dignity. Let us now examine in detail how Jesus wishes to exercise His mission of redemption in us.

As we have seen, Jesus is priest, prophet and king. He has been sent among men to redeem them by His sacrifice, to teach them in truth, to accomplish the Kingdom of God in them. The glorious Christ wishes this threefold mission to continue on earth. Since this work still remains to be done, He appeals for the collaboration of His priestly People. Hence, our vocation. We must live in union with Jesus who lives invisibly in the midst of

His People: (1) In union with Christ, offering
sacrifice in the midst of His people; (2) In
union with Christ teaching in the midst of His
People; (3) In union with Christ ruling in the
midst of His People.

1. LIFE IN UNION WITH CHRIST OFFERING SACRIFICE IN THE MIDST OF HIS PEOPLE

The priestly People must live in union with Jesus in
order to offer a spiritual worship for God's glory
and the expiation of the world's sins. For this reason
it has the duty of leading a holy life of prayer and
Christian abnegnation.

We can approach God with great confidence, for by virtue of our Baptism and
Confirmation we have, so to speak, official
credentials with His Majesty, though our personal sins make us unworthy of this. However,
the Father of all mercy "has blessed us with
every spiritual blessing on high in Christ.
Even as He chose us in Him before the foundation of the world, that we should be holy
and without blemish in His sight in love. He
predestined us to be adopted through Jesus
Christ as His sons, according to the purpose
of His will, unto the praise of the glory of His
grace, with which He has favored us in His
beloved Son. In Him we have redemption
through His blood, the remission of sins." [1]

With confidence in the mercy of the Father, in intimate union with Jesus Christ, consumed with a desire of giving glory to God, with our eyes turned to the Lord, we must strive to make of our whole life a cult of homage. Such a life will be theocentric, not egocentric. We shall strive to live in the holy presence of God. We will pour forth our gratitude for the magnanimity, the courage, the devotion, the piety, the faith, hope, love, and all the other virtues that the Holy Spirit, the Divine Artist, is working out in the heart of mankind. We shall be sensitive to every sign of His goodness. But above all, the life of the priestly People will endeavor to be a marveling look at, and a deep consideration of, the splendor of the Father's glory, a constant song of praise in behalf of all creation.

Some in the liturgical Office, others in the breviary of their daily Christian work—all will sing with the psalmist: "Give thanks to the Lord, invoke His name; make known among the nations His deeds. . . Glory in His name; rejoice, O hearts that seek the Lord! Look to the Lord in His strength; seek to serve Him constantly: Recall the wondrous deeds that He has wrought. His portents, and the judgments He has uttered." [2]

Members of the royal priesthood must become interior men. Their first preoccupation must be that taught by Jesus Himself: "Father, hallowed be Thy name, Thy kingdom come, Thy will be done on earth as it is in heaven." [3] But this royal priesthood has also the mission of bearing the burden of the sins of the world together with Christ. Priests, religious, and laymen—all are thrown into the battle and carry the burden of heavy, engrossing, apostolic labors. You cannot lose sight of the fact that in the eyes of the eternal Father, you also are "the Lamb of God, who takes away the sins of the world." [4]

When you see your brothers overwhelmed by poverty or nailed to a bed of suffering, or the object of derision, persecution, and martyrdom, you must say to yourselves: they are fulfilling their priestly role. When the silent Church, crucified with Christ, is described for us, you must say: They are offering their sacrifice. Their example must urge us to greater generosity and greater fidelity in the mission of expiation. May yours be the soul of priest and victim! You must endure "the burden of the day's heat" [5] in your professional and apostolic life, with the intention of making it reparation for sin.

Remember the words of St. Paul: "I rejoice now in the sufferings I bear for your

sake; and what is lacking of the sufferings of
Christ I fill up in my flesh for His body, which
is the Church; whose minister I have become
in virtue of the office that God has given me
in your regard. For I am to preach the word
of God fully. . . It is Christ we preach, admon-
ishing every man and teaching every man in
all wisdom, that we may present every man
perfect in Christ Jesus. At this, too, I work
and strive, according to the power which He
mightily exerts in me." [6]

Thus, throughout each day you must "present your bodies as a sacrifice, living, holy,
pleasing to God—your spiritual service. And
be not conformed to this world, but be trans-
formed in the newness of your mind, that you
may discern what is the good and acceptable
and perfect will of God." [7] You will gradually be able to discover this will of God con-
naturally,[8] so to speak, for "the Spirit also
helps our weakness. For we do not know
what we should pray for as we ought, but the
Spirit Himself pleads for us with unutterable
groanings." [9]

The People of God have no right to live a
surface existence; their life must be lived in
depth. Their mission is to form part of a
priestly community whose whole life is a cult,
a service of adoration and gratitude, a holo-

caust of intercession and reparation. Let us overcome, therefore, our parochial individualism, our sloth, our cowardice, and make offering in fraternal union in Christ and with Him. "Hold fast what thou hast, that no one receive thy crown. He who overcomes, I will make him a pillar in the temple of my God, and never more shall he go outside. And I will write upon him the name of my God, and the name of the city of my God—the new Jerusalem, which comes down out of heaven from my God—and my new name. He who has an ear, let him hear what the Spirit says to the churches." [10]

2. LIFE IN UNION WITH CHRIST TEACHING IN THE MIDST OF HIS PEOPLE

(a) *Christian Witness*

The priestly mission of offering spiritual service together with Christ is not limited to prayer and expiation. Following the example of Jesus, the People of God must add the offering of their constant concern to know, to proclaim, to live, and to defend the Christian message, the Word of God.

Spreading the gospel is in a special way a part of Christian worship. St. Paul said: "For God is my witness, whom I serve in my spirit in the gospel of His Son." [1] This priesthood of ours obliges us to take the initiative in making known the gospel to our neighbors. We have received the commission of bearing Christian witness. How could our priestly community dare make its offering, if it did not do everything in its power to bring Christ's message to the knowledge of mankind and so live that its life be agreeable to God?

But this witness does not spring merely from our lips—our whole life brings to our neighbors the message of the Lord. This royal worship will not be sincere if the People of God fail to show, by their acts, fidelity to the message that Christ has come to reveal. We must present ourselves in the temple of the Eternal One, clothed with those qualities of which Christ has deigned to give us an example. Thus the Father would have us. Has He not "predestined" us "to become conformed to the image of His Son, that He should be the firstborn among many brethren." [2]

In all the events of life we must ask ourselves: How would Christ have acted in this circumstance? We must constantly strive to conform our attitudes to the ideal of Christ and to radiate the splendor of the Lord our God. The Gospel must be part of our life. This is the only way in which our message will carry weight and our life will be pleasing to Christ and to Him who sent Him. In fact,

Jesus Himself strives to mold our life unto His likeness, and wishes us to learn "to practice the truth in love." [3] It is He who constantly sends His Spirit so that our life may conform to His message, and that instead of being ashamed of His gospel, we may be faithful witnesses of it and its courageous defenders.[4]

To bear witness to Christ is the mission not only of the whole community of the People of God but of each individual Christian.[5] It is a natural and spontaneous result of the fact that those who are baptized together form a corporate priestly body. No special designation is needed, no high mandate is required in order to apply oneself to it. This responsibility derives from the fact that one is a Christian. When we imitate Christ, those about us see it, and they cannot fail to be impressed by the beauty of Christianity. A Christian is bound to present this spontaneous radiation to his neighbors: "You are the light of the world. . . Neither do men light a lamp and put it under the measure . . . let your light shine before men, in order that they may see your good works and give glory to your Father in heaven." [6]

A Christian must desire that his very presence should become a stimulus for good and a blessing for his family, his neighborhood, the places where he works and takes his recreation. He must consider the tools of his work —his body and his heart—as sacred objects that Christ wishes to use in order to elevate the human and Christian level of his surroundings.

But the apostolic mission of the People of God is certainly not restricted to the proclamation of the Word of God. The echo of that Word should penetrate profoundly and reach far and wide to all those whom Jesus came to save.

(b) *Apostolic Mission of the People of God*

It is the duty of the People of God to proclaim the Christian message through the power of the Spirit and the abundance of its own apostolic enterprises.

The apostolate is actually a revelation of God. It is a theophany of the Word that speaks so as to make known the plan of salvation to men. This Word makes known the Father, and communicates the message of salvation along with the condition needed for participation in it.

This communication of the message, being "the Word of God," is the essence of the formal mission of the Lord. Now, the plan of salvation is such that it calls for the continuation of Christ's message to the world in us, His People. Our mission is to proclaim the message of salvation and to make known that God is love, that He has sent His Son, who has risen from the dead and that His Spirit dwells among us.

God's plan demands that henceforth Christ speak to the world in His Church. How would the world hear God's word if we did not make ourselves its messengers? [1] How can unbelievers, indifferent Christians, those near and far—how can they hear the message of love, if we fail to make it known to them?

We are negligent in the most elementary of our duties if, by our silence, we allow to slip away an opportunity to make known even the least portion of the message of love. The first Christians were profoundly convinced about this. They felt obliged to bear witness, and were driven to speak of the Word, to declare their belief in the resurrection and the descent of the Holy Spirit. St. Peter says: "You are . . . a purchased people; that you may proclaim the perfections of Him who has called you out of darkness into His marvelous light." [2] This is the reason for our existence, the task before us.

When Christ said to His apostles: "Come follow Me, and I will make you fishers of men," [3] He assigned to them a hard task, which they were to perform as "unprofitable servants," no doubt, but at the same time making use of all their talents. The fisherman does not wait for the fish to come, but strives to capture them. While the Christian labors with God, throws out his net into the water "in His name," and works in the "power of the Spirit," he must, nevertheless, yearn for an abundant haul, and must devote to this end the best of himself, his intelligence, imagination and other human endowments. Unquestionably the Christian message must be proclaimed, but this proclamation has to be supplemented by reflection and planned efforts so as to induce others to follow Christ. Truth endeavors to make itself known, and real charity, which must animate the Body of Christ, cannot rest until all men have accepted the spiritual blessings offered by the Redeemer. A mission of proclaiming and persuading is committed to the royal priesthood of the People of God. [4]

The apostolate is the duty of the People as a whole. All the members must foster in their hearts the concerns about which St. Paul speaks: ". . . my daily pressing anxiety, the care of all the Churches! Who is weak, and I am not weak? Who is made to stumble, and I am not inflamed?" [5] There must be a commitment of the whole Body of Christ, and each individual must apply his strength and his resources so that the heavenly Father may be known and glorified in Christian lands of long standing as well as in the missions.

At this point, however, a word of caution is in order. Efforts to spread Christ's doctrine would not be an act of "spiritual worship," and would be unworthy of the royal priesthood, if they had the earmarks of purely human propaganda.

The witness of a Christian is a religious frame of mind and a supernatural form of action. Christ's apostle devotes himself to this work, not to please men, nor to gain a reputation or acquire standing. It is the love of God that drives him to it. This witness is the overflow of love. Of course, the means he uses will not go counter to the laws of psychology, but they are, first and foremost, supernatural means: a lively faith, firm hope, and a deep respect for the sacred deposit he is passing on to others. "God, as it were, appealing through us." [6]

In another place St. Paul sets down the golden rule for this testimony: "And I, brethren, when I came to you, did not come with pretentious speech or wisdom, announcing unto you the witness to Christ. For I determined not to know anything among you, except Jesus Christ, and Him crucified. And I was with you in weakness and in fear and in much trembling. And my speech and my preaching were not in the persuasive words of wisdom, but in the demonstration of the Spirit and of power, that your faith might rest, not on the wisdom of men, but on the power of God." [7]

Let each one of us examine himself. What is the value of my witness? Is it an act of worship or am I "as sounding brass or a tinkling cymbal"? [8] If our speech is not a supernatural preaching, it has no place in Christ who teaches in His People.

(c) *Christian Tolerance*

The People of God must be animated by a deep respect for, and a genuine charity toward, all those who do not share their religious convictions, and they must refrain from all forms of intolerance.

Though we tell you to be fishers of men, we must also warn you against that false zeal that goes by the name of intolerance. We refer to ill-advised proselytism and fanatical propaganda methods, which make use of flattery, money, force and intimidation, whether openly or covertly, in order to make converts. We must absolutely avoid such methods, not only because we ourselves would not like to be the victims of such procedures, but because charity and the respect due to the human person as well as the very nature of the act of faith, preclude this sort of thing.

We must show respect and charity toward those who do not yet share our faith, remembering that Christian tolerance [1] is a frame of mind that issues from justice and charity. If we are to convince somebody of the truth of the Catholic faith, this will be accomplished by prayer, our witness to the faith, and calm persuasion, setting forth arguments clearly and objectively. The unassailable dignity of the human person demands our respect, even when a person is mistaken but in good faith. The very fact that someone is honestly trying to settle his conscience is already a proof of a basically good moral disposition. Furthermore, when a man is sincere, absolute fidelity to his conscience is the only sound approach to truth.

Undoubtedly, we must love all men for whom Christ shed His blood. Charity bids us wish the advancement of our neighbor. But this desire to have others embrace the faith should forbid us from having recourse to any means that would violate another's spiritual privacy. It would be absurd to act otherwise.

The act of faith is primarily the result of divine grace. Surely we do not want to force God's hand! On the human side, the act of faith is a free assent to the will of God. If the assent is not free, the act of faith is nonexistent, and the so-called conversion obtained by such tactics is a mere parody.

The foregoing principles have an absolute and timeless value. However, at present there is special reason for underscoring them because of the particular situation in which the Church finds herself today: that is, in an ever more closely-knit world in which all sorts of convictions confront one another. It would cause serious harm to the spread of Christianity, to the good name and the influence of the Catholic Church, and to harmony among peoples, if, in a given situation, these directives were not followed.

While saying that you must always be tolerant toward those who do not share our religious convictions, we are quite aware that you yourselves are not infrequently the victims of the intolerance of others. Such is the intolerance of those who deny us the right and the liberty to believe with absolute certitude to the exclusion of skepticism and doubt, in the supernatural truths revealed by Christ. In the name of tolerance they are intolerant toward

us. Then there are those who oppose us with
haughty disdain, and charge that we are true
to the faith only because of insufficient reflection or defective education, by our fear of
breaking with outmoded traditions, or of in-
curring what they call the thunder of the
priestly caste. Above all, there is the anony-
mous persecutor, namely, the materialistic and
atheistic milieu, that tends to level everything,
and to immerse everything in an ever-growing
immorality.

It is our duty to tell you that even amid mis-
understanding and persecution, our hearts
must be full of charity toward all men without exception: "Love your enemies, do good
to those who hate you, and pray for those who
persecute and calumniate you, so that you
may be children of your Father in heaven,
who makes His sun to rise on the good and the
evil, and sends rain on the just and the un-
just. . . . You therefore are to be perfect, even
as your heavenly Father is perfect." [2] This
does not mean that every Christian should not
be concerned for brothers who are in danger.
There are times when Christians must unite,
even in secular spheres, for the defense of the
rights of the human person, the Christian
conscience, and the liberty of the Church of
Christ. Moreover, wisdom and true charity

bid us not to wait for persecution before
organizing.

It will always be the mission of the People
of God to discourage and anticipate every
threat of persecution by creating, in all social
strata a public opinion devoted to liberty and
respect for the rights of man and religion.

3. LIFE IN UNION WITH CHRIST RULING IN THE MIDST OF HIS PEOPLE

The royal priesthood entrusted with the spiritual
worship of the true God, Father of all men, cannot
restrict its spiritual offerings to prayer, expiation,
and Christian witness. It will also offer to God its
efforts to bring all under one head, Christ. It will do
this by working in a spirit of faith, hope, and
charity, in accord with the duties of one's state of
life, toward an ever growing unification, humanization, redemption, and consecration of the world.

(a) *The Kingship of Christ*

Humanity seeks progress and happiness. It
is a universal urge. The way to pursue this
is clearly indicated by the law written in the
natural tendencies of all creation. By calling
it into existence, God has given to every being
the law of balance and unity. Every individual creature seeks to preserve its unity. Every
inferior being is oriented toward a higher
order, and is destined for the service of man.

Man is called upon freely to achieve the balance and harmony of his natural tendencies, to subject them to reason, and to advance with all men toward ever greater consciousness and unity. Man cannot achieve real happiness unless he brings his actual conduct into line with the plan of the Creator until, after his earthly probation, he will be finally united to his last end, God Himself.

This equilibrium is endangered by sin, whose essence it is to destroy man's unity. Rebellion against God's plans brings about man's enslavement to matter and to his passions. This is soon enough followed by pangs of conscience, disruption of the family, insecurity, social conflicts, wars, and the break with God.

As you know, Jesus came to restore the unity that had been destroyed. His mission was the re-establishment of the created order's orientation toward its Creator, the raising up of fallen mankind, and the restoration of union between man and God. But the work entrusted to Him by His Father does not stop there. The Son of God was to open up new possibilities to mankind and to the world. Man was called to become a son of God, to live in Christ, to find a place in a mystical society of which Jesus would be the Head, and which would

be the family of God, the People of God. But
it was not only to man that Christ would communicate His life: He was also, in a way, to
confer it on things. All creation was to be
directed toward this divine end. Step by step
it was to recover the order that was willed by
the Creator, until it would finally serve man as
a springboard that would enable him to reach
his ultimate destiny.

In this way the new order was to come
about, "this His good pleasure God purposed
in Him, to be dispensed in the fullness of the
times: to re-establish all things in Christ, both
those in the heavens and those on earth." [1]

This is the kingship of Christ. The essence
of royal power is not subject to others. Its
prerogative is to orient persons and things
toward the ends it proposes to attain. Jesus
has merited this power as Head and Savior of
humanity. He has the royal power of making
laws destined to transform fallen creation; He
exercises executive power, and leads things
and men toward their end; He has judiciary
power and will pronounce final sentence at
the end of time. After having merited this
power by His life on earth, Jesus will effectively establish it by having all creation share,
step by step, in His resurrection and in His
glorification in heaven.

"Therefore, we are debtors, not to the flesh, that we should live according to the flesh, for if you live according to the flesh you will die; but if by the spirit you put to death the deeds of the flesh, you will live. For whoever are led by the Spirit of God, they are the Sons of God. Now you have not received a spirit of bondage, so as to be again in fear, but you have received a spirit of adoption as sons, by virtue of which we cry, 'Abba! Father!' The Spirit Himself gives testimony to our spirit that we are sons of God. But if we are sons, we are heirs also: heirs indeed of God, and joint heirs with Christ, provided, however, we suffer with Him that we may also be glorified with Him." [2]

(b) *A Royal People*

Christ appeals to the whole priestly community of His chosen People to spread His kingdom effectively throughout creation. He wishes to establish His kingship through you. By collaboration with Jesus in freeing yourselves from the chains of sin, you establish the rule of Christ. By accepting the sacrifices implied in the duties of your state of life, in a co-redemptive spirit, and by adding thereto voluntary sacrifices, you work for the triumph of the crucified God. By giving to matter its real dignity, making it serve man's true interests, you realize at one and the same time the plan for which Christ has made the offering of His life. By making use of sensible signs and of the words instituted by Christ, you can even — under certain circumstances — be the ministers of Christ, in conferring on the People of God the sacramental grace of Baptism and Marriage. This fidelity to the duties of your state of life is a spiritual offering of your priesthood. It makes, so to speak, your professional life, your family, social, political, and international life, an uninterrupted tribute which, day in and day out, you present, in Christ, to the eternal Father.[1]

We urge you to become more and more aware of this aspect of your priestly vocation in the midst of the world. If you accomplish your daily tasks with the desire of following Christ's doctrine and of spreading its influence, there will be no opposition between your religious life and your task on earth. You will be living an incarnate Christianity; you will be following the royal road of the Cross.

Continue, then, trying to create an evermore favorable atmosphere everywhere — where you work, where you take your recreation, and especially where you live. In connection with the last point, remember [2] how desirable it is that each "neighborhood" should become a small Christian community where all know and help one another. Experience has shown that it is not so difficult to re-animate this neighborly spirit. If each neighborhood becomes a cell of Christian living, the parish will soon become an organic whole. Under these circumstances, a thousand and one details of daily life will make each parishioner feel that the great Christian family shares his cares, and does not leave him to himself. Strive, then, to create in the diocese a public opinion favorable to the Christian organization of the different areas of life. Do not be satisfied with an apostolate in which your efforts are scattered. "Organizing ourselves in charity" constitutes the most effective and peaceful opposition we can offer to certain forms of intolerance directed against us.

Men and women, wherever Providence has placed you, that is where you have to live as faithful subjects of your King in heaven. Catholicism is not an easy religion. You know what the Master meant when He said: "Do not think that I have come to send peace upon the earth; I have come to bring a sword, not peace." [3] Your duty is to withstand all the attractions of a non-Christian spirit that would water down the vigor of your Christianity. The salt must not lose its savor. Remember the service you do to all mankind by being the agents of a Christian renewal.

Let men show in their conduct a balanced masculinity, a sense of sacrifice in their work, and a true team spirit. Let women, following the example of the Virgin Mary, show by their constant affability and their complete generosity that they are faithful collaborators upon whom the Lord may rely. Let youth draw inspiration from the Christian ideal, in order to renew a society urgently in need of being strengthened and rejuvenated. If your life is truly based on self-renunciation, you will contribute your share to the consecration of the world.

The responsibility of all men, as members of the royal priesthood, imposes on them the duty of inspiring and bringing about the advancement and protection of all the brethren whose faith is endangered.

The social nature of man and his participation in the life of the Body of Christ call for a certain atmosphere or communal spirit. In the apostolate we all too frequently forget that it is not enough to evangelize individual persons. It is equally urgent to create a favorable atmosphere in which the disciple of Jesus Christ can feel that he is understood and encouraged by others, or, at any rate, by some of his brethren in the faith. Christ has placed each of the faithful "in the midst" of others. There he must labor and radiate among them, so as to make each one of the faithful near to him feel that he is not an isolated being, but is surrounded and protected by prayer, affection, and the fellowship of many others. Concern for the establishment of a truly Christian environment, and systematic collaboration in the apostolate, are simply the logical consequence of the fact that we constitute a *whole* in Christ, and that we all share in His royal priesthood.

The exalted task that God has entrusted to every human being is to make the world a better place to live in for mankind, and to put it more and more at the service of man. The Creator calls on the insight of our minds, the strength of our bodies, and the goodness of our hearts, to create a form of life in which man may attain complete human development and the most perfect union with Christ.

Christians, then, must collaborate in the making of such a world. They must do so in union with their brethren in the faith, but they must also strive to collaborate with others. The disciples of Christ must associate themselves with every man of good will, not

only in the shoulder-to-shoulder tasks of daily
life and work, but also on the organizational
level. They must take part in the activity
of groups established to help them in the
realization of their temporal mission. Whatever their place in society, their secular commitment must contribute to the creation of an
atmosphere favorable for the human and
Christian advancement of all those with whom
they are associated.

In the first place, the Christian knows that
he has been created to the image of God.[4]
Now God is the Creator and Lord of His work.
And so man, inasmuch as he is made to the
image of God, is also a creator and lord of
creation, dependent on, and at the service of,
God. This is why Scripture says that God gave
man the commission to have dominion over
the earth [5] and to fill the earth and subdue it.[6]
In other words, God has placed in the world
resources and potentialities, and in man talents
and capabilities for advancement, which cannot achieve their full flowering without the
watchful care and active contribution of man.

As the image of God, man will accomplish
his mission of lord and creator—as a secon-
dary, free cause—by transforming the world
more and more from a purely natural place to
a cultural and truly human environment. By

this very fact, work, whereby man takes command of the earth and develops himself, takes on a religious significance. Man must work convinced that he is working with God,[7] that the daily task to which he consecrates himself is truly an *Opus Dei*, and that when he is conscious of the religious significance of his daily work, he is realizing St. Paul's mandate to do everything for the glory of God.[8]

Moreover, the great, new commandment given to His disciples by Jesus,[9] which He will take as the decisive criterion on the day of judgment,[10] is that of fraternal charity. Now the inner significance and primary objective of work and professional activity is service to the community. So true is this that a profession that makes no contribution to society must necessarily fall into disuse. For a Christian this means that his fraternal charity which, in order to be truly such, must advance the good of others (*velle bonum alicui*), becomes incarnate in a special and fundamental way in his work, or in the profession he exercises from day to day in the society of his fellow men. A Christian who does not take the practice of his profession seriously, does not deserve the name of Christian,[11] because he neglects what should be the practical exercise of charity. For a Christian, the exercise of one's profession has a religious meaning, because it incarnates the most essential Christian value: charity.

The two following principles define the place of the Christian in the sphere of secular values.

In the first place, to be faithful to the purpose of His Creator, he must develop his natural gifts. Revelation does not indicate to him the ways and means of performing his work in the domain of what, for lack of a suitable term, we call "culture" and "civilization." To meet the scientific and technological requirements of his mission on earth, he must put to use the natural talents God has given him.

Secondly, he must be faithful to the law of charity which he has received from his Savior. If he lives by this charity, he will be the more fit to consecrate himself to his task in the service of the community. The dynamism of charity will help him to discover and find truly human solutions to the problems that arise in society. History shows that men gifted with a great charity have found a practical way to better the living conditions of their fellow men. They are the source of whatever progress may be achieved by way of better institutions and laws that are more and more worthy of man.

As you gradually spread the kingdom of Christ, you will restore balance and harmony in all creation. A greater humanization of labor will result. New inventions, technological advances, a more efficient organization will lessen the physical effort in work, recompense ability, and make the energy expended less onerous and more worthy of man. More humane working conditions will encourage greater productivity and social progress. There is no doubt that shorter working hours, guaranteed vacations, payment for leaves of absence, insurance against unemployment, sickness and disability, family allowances and old-age pensions, will certainly enable men to develop their intellectual faculties and open their minds to the beauties of nature, art and culture in general.[12]

If you promote this process of humanization and spiritualization according to Christian principles and in union with Christ, your efforts will be crowned by a wider and deeper participation of the whole secular order in the sphere of the spiritual. Balance and harmony, humanization and spiritualization will lead to the consecration of the world. If they are performed in union with the Master, all man's actions will be animated by the resolve to consecrate oneself to the glory of God. These actions will then take on an eschatological character, and prepare the way for the period of Christ's final triumph: "For we know that all creation groans and travails in pain until now. And not only it, but we ourselves also who have the first-fruits of the Spirit—we ourselves groan within ourselves, waiting for the adoption as sons, the redemption of our body. For in hope were we saved." [13]

As we close this letter on the sublimity and mission of the People of God, we beseech the Holy Spirit to lead you to understand that your life must assume more and more a priestly character.

Do not withdraw within yourselves absorbed by the pursuit of your own special interests, even spiritual interests. Put aside your ego, and become aware of the sacred character of your life as a Christian, its consecration and its obligations.

Narrow individualism must find no place in the apostolate. At the present moment, there is a tendency among the young to prefer a free, uncommitted, individual apostolate, according to each one's natural dispositions and preferences; a certain dilettantism that is on its guard against all organized effort or definite commitment. May the consciousness of belonging to the royal priesthood of Christ make you see the need for collective and organized action in order to teach the People of God to live and to strengthen its life of union with Christ, Priest, Teacher and King.

The eyes of God are on you. He has made you sharers in the priesthood of His Son. You are to take part in His mission of Victim. Let your life be one of service in the worship He continues to give the Father with total devotion.

Offer the Father the worship of your prayer, abnegation, and Christian witness; and finally, make an offering of your efforts to orient men and things to God "that God may be all in all."[14]

Each one of you is called to this sublime mission; and this is the role, too, of the People of God. The Catholic Church is a priestly community. All its members, whatever their rank or their function, are in possession, basically and forever, of this vocation to the priesthood of the Lord. Even those who become ministers by ordination—and this will be the subject of some remarks in the second part— even bishops and priests of the ministry, have, outside the exercise of their ecclesiastical functions, duties and responsibilities common to the whole People of God.

III
Religious and Members of Secular Institutes

Since Jesus continues His royal priesthood in each one of us, we have the obligation of sharing His thoughts in all things. Following His example we must love His Church and wish to see her beautiful in every respect, for according to St. Paul, "Christ also loved the Church, and delivered Himself up for her, that He might sanctify her . . . in order that he might present to Himself the Church in all her glory, not having spot or wrinkle or any such thing, but that she might be holy and without blemish." [1]

It must be our constant concern to make holy Mother Church more and more like her divine Head, for it is by sharing His thoughts, His ways, and His attitudes that she will become great and holy. Consequently, we must approve and love all the assignments to which the Father invites members of the royal priesthood. Some will have to direct their efforts primarily to the duties of family life and to augment its Christian radiance; they represent Christ living in Nazareth. Others will apply themselves more specially to works of mercy; they represent in the Church, Christ going about the world and doing good. Others reflect the image of Christ healing the sick, or Christ teaching, or again Christ consoling the afflicted and living in the midst of men. All these forms of life are a sharing in the life of Christ as priest, prophet, and king, but the emphasis in each case varies in accordance with each one's special vocation.[2]

However, among the People of God there is a vocation superior to all the various forms of the lay state: This is the religious state [3] and that of members of secular institutes.

There are men and women whom God calls to give themselves to Him out of a love or charity that excludes the goods that laymen seek by the very fact of their human vocation. Laymen are called to love God with their whole heart, with their whole soul, and with their whole mind; but this total offering of their hearts to God does not exclude, or rather, it includes, a family to be raised and a position to be held in the human community. In the case of those whom God destines for a life of consecration, the charity to which they are called must not only take hold of their whole heart, but must also embrace God alone.[4]

The better to achieve this singular charity, they make an uninterrupted sacrifice of their whole life by means of the evangelical counsels which they seal with a vow.

By the vow of chastity, in the interests of a greater love, they deny themselves the joys of an earthly union, and of family life sanctified by marriage. In their desire for an exclusive love, they bind themselves to Christ crucified, to make reparation for sins of the flesh and all the sins of men. By the vow of poverty they imitate Christ who did not wish to take a place among the great ones of the earth, those who are singled out by their riches and who so easily become hard and unapproachable. Their undistinguished lives are not only a holocaust, but are also a reminder of the Christian ideal: "If anyone wishes to come after Me, let him deny himself, and take up his cross, and follow Me. . . He who loses his life for My sake will find it." [5]

They also seek to make their witness absolute and exclusive by their voluntary dependence on the authority instituted by Christ. For their vow—or commitment—of obedience is an act of self-identification, definitive in intention and then progressively realized with

Christ, whose surrender to the Father was a total one. Their life is thus pre-eminently a sharing in the life of immolation of Christ, the Priest. It is the most unconditional form of human offering among the People of God.

A "consecrated" life is also a life offered to Christ the Prophet with the intent of bearing witness to Him. Whatever the form of this witness, all religious and all members of secular institutes—not only those engaged in the active life, but also the most strictly contemplative—are apostolic. As His Holiness, the late Pope Pius XII said: "Let nuns who are cloistered realize that their vocation is completely and totally apostolic." [6] In fact, those who are "consecrated" are persons placed in the midst of the world, who, in the eyes of the onlooker, should clearly be seen to take the gospel seriously.

This is especially true of religious, whose very attire is often in itself a public declaration of their faith. They live as a group, gathered together in community for mutual support in every difficulty, and in order to make their witness more effective. They prove in this way that an evangelical life is not only possible as an ideal, but can also be realized in practice. Their life is a reminder addressed to the world. Those who observe them realize that they have said to themselves: "Let us therefore go forth to Him outside the camp, bearing His reproach for here we have no permanent city, but we seek for the city that is to come. Through Him, therefore, let us offer up a sacrifice of praise always to God, that is, fruit of lips praising His name." [7]

Unquestionably, these consecrated persons are unsurpassed in their cooperation with Christ for the establishment of His kingdom. Their lives are oriented toward God. Their rule, their customs, their spiritual practices, the fruit of immemorial experience accumulated in lives lived for God, are certainly the surest way toward the unification, spiritualization, and progressive consecration of their lives.

Surely, one cannot compute the influence exercised by them in the world's journey to God—teaching the young, caring for the sick and handicapped, the newborn and aged, house-visiting, and the direct apostolate. What must be the importance for the world's salvation, and the kingdom of Christ, of those torrents of prayers and sacrifice that rise up from all these convents and monasteries, like a flood whose waves beat insistently at the gates of heaven! The Church knows best how much she needs these men and women who are unconditionally and directly pledged to lend her their generous cooperation and whole-hearted support.

While waiting to take their place in the midst of the People of God, before the throne where Christ the King will be in His ultimate Kingdom, those "consecrated" persons, along with all those in the world who live in consecrated celibacy, already fulfill in themselves, while still on earth, the eschatological vision of the Apocalypse: "And I saw, and behold, the Lamb was standing upon Mount Sion, and with him a hundred and forty-four thousand having His name and the name of His Father written on their foreheads. And I heard a voice from heaven. . . And they were singing as it were a new song before the throne, and before the four living creatures and the elders; and no one could learn the song except those hundred and forty-four thousand, who have been purchased from the earth. These are they who were not defiled with women; for they are virgins. These follow the Lamb wherever He goes. These were purchased from among men, first-fruits unto God and unto the Lamb." [8]

It is not surprising that our Lord gives visible blessings to dioceses in which a large number of the faithful have consecrated their lives to the task He has most at heart. Unquestionably, it is a great joy for the pastor of a diocesan family to be able to accept and bless each year, in the name of Holy Church and of Christ, the public vows and pledges of fresh recruits who answer the call of Christ, and also to enroll them in the army of His apostles. The members themselves of the diocesan family also have reason to rejoice sincerely at the sight of this added beauty of Christ's Body, and of this proof of the power of His grace.

Our times are not favorable to higher vocations. Let us pray that the splendor of Christ may not be dimmed in the world. May our young people who are so religious-minded and profound not let themselves be sullied with the mud of the wayside. Priests, religious and laymen, the problem of vocations is the concern of all of you. If some day Christ comes and knocks at the door of your heart, your family, or your organization—do not be deaf to His call.

Part Two

THE PEOPLE OF GOD
AND THEIR PASTORS

Serving the People of God

The priestly ministry is a service whose soul is Christ. The People of God have a right to call on it for everything they need during their stay on earth so that they, too, will live in union with Christ when He offers sacrifice, teaches, and rules.

Up to this point we have set forth the activities of the People of God. Jesus operates in them. However, it is not His wish that His Mystical Body be a mere passive recipient of His influence. He could never be satisfied with a purely passive attitude. Jesus continues His priesthood in the whole Christian community. In it and through it He offers to the Father a worship that is pleasing to Him. In and through it He spreads His gospel. In it and through it He brings about the consecration of the world. It is wrong to suppose that according to Catholic doctrine part of the faithful are reduced to a purely passive state. It is loose thinking to claim that the faithful are merely a flock of sheep resigned to being meekly and forcibly led by their shepherds. This you clearly understand: All the baptized without exception united together, constitute the royal priesthood of Christ.

Going a step further—in the heart of this priestly organism there are some members with a special share in the priesthood of Christ. In the second part of this pastoral letter we shall speak of the ministerial priesthood —Pope, bishops, and priests. It is not our intention to give you a doctrinal explanation of Holy Orders. Our purpose in speaking of them is to show that this ministerial priesthood was instituted by Christ, so that the People of God may be better able to achieve the mission entrusted to them.

We will first give a general description of the part played by Pope, bishops, and priests. Next we will show how Christ sends them forth as pastors, with the mandate to assist the People of God in the practice of their spiritual worship, of their witness, and in the consecration of the world.

I
The
Priestly
Ministry

They have the power to enable the people to live in union with Christ, to invigorate their priestly action, to coordinate efforts and make up for their shortcomings.

In their life on earth, the People of God are in the formative stage. By virtue of their share in the priesthood of Christ, all members of the Body must combine their influence and coordinate their efforts so that His word and His grace may penetrate the world. But is there not some authority entrusted with the organization of the Church's apostolic work? Christ has not left the continuation of His work exclusively to the charismatic direction of the Holy Spirit. Was it possible that a purely charismatic phase of the apostolate should succeed the first years of the Christian era, when salvation was achieved by the visible sign of the Incarnate Word's earthly life?

Jesus Christ has instituted in His Church a visible organ—a sacrament from the beginning, personally involved with the apostolic action of His people—to be the efficacious sign of His truth, His saving will. He wished that human intermediaries should be entrusted with the task of putting the means of salvation at the disposal of His people. He has given His pastors the mandate of helping the priesthood of the faithful in the accomplishment of its mission. He has created an indispensable organ to guarantee completion of the mission entrusted to the community of the faithful.

1. POPE AND BISHOPS

The episcopal College in union with the Pope and under his direction is responsible for the extension of the means of salvation and for preaching the word of God. They must bring about in the world an upsurge of charity.

"All power in heaven and on earth has been given to Me. Go, therefore, and make disciples of all nations, baptizing them in the name of the Father, and of the Son, and of the Holy Spirit, teaching them to observe all that I have commanded you; and behold, I am with you all days, even unto the consummation of the world." [1] Such is the solemn mission of the Twelve and the charter of the ministerial apostolate of the apostolic college during the first centuries. And "whatever you bind on earth shall be bound also in heaven; and whatever you loose on earth shall be loosed also in heaven." [2] The apostolic College, it is true, founded the Church, and for this reason each of the apostles had personal prerogatives that could not be handed on. But the apostolic college itself also truly inaugurated the hierarchical framework of the Church, which was to last from century to century in the episcopal college. Moreover, it was to a member of the apostolic college that our Lord addressed these solemn words: "Thou art Peter, and upon this rock I will build My Church, and the gates of hell shall not prevail against it. And I will give thee the keys of the kingdom of heaven; and whatever thou shalt bind on earth shall be bound in heaven, and whatever thou shalt loose on earth shall be loosed in heaven." [3] And a little later we hear the words "feed My sheep" [4] and "do thou . . . strengthen thy brethren." [5]

The Sovereign Pontiff and his brethren the bishops, entrusted with different individual Churches, have received the fullness of the priesthood. The Holy Spirit rests on them. Since they have been elevated to watch over the deposit of grace, they are responsible for the spread of salvation. As friends and confidants of Christ, they may not rest as long as there are men who are not yet living stones in the temple of the Lord.

Pope and bishops are to show equal zeal in the ministry of the word, "that the word of the Lord may run and be glorified." [6] They possess an active and dynamic force in their teaching and juridical power. Christ communicates to their minds, hearts and words a concern to teach men to lead a life worthy of the Lord, to be fruitful in all manner of good works, and to grow in the knowledge of God, "completely strengthened through His glorious power." [7]

Finally, Christ makes use of them that the rule of the Father may come, and that His will be done on earth as in heaven. To achieve this, they strive to stir up in the world a yearning for truth and charity.[8] They are animators, not merely administrators. For amid the hard facts of this earthly existence, the kingdom of Christ must not be institutionalized or reduced to the formalities of a legal façade. It must be a life-current permeating everything, an enterprising and pervasive charity that strives to become a universal movement of mutual and fraternal respect.

2. PRIESTS

On the local level, Christ continues to live as a Pastor among His own through the agency of priests who are ministers of the faith, of Christian hope, and of divine charity.

Christ gave to the apostolic college the power of appointing collaborators to follow the needs of local communities. As the need arises in his diocese, a bishop is authorized to call to his aid men chosen by the Lord and with the necessary qualifications, that they may help him to be God's representative among men and men's representative before God. There is only one ministerial priesthood, and this the bishop possesses in its plenitude. A priest shares in the same priesthood in a limited measure.

In the person of the priest, Jesus continues to live in the midst of His People for all to see. Through him Jesus addresses His invitation to men: "Follow Me." Christians—young and old—understand that it is the priest's duty to live in the midst of his flock. They have given him the title of pastor, curate, chaplain, assistant, and Father. Before all else, the flock looks for a man with a heart, not a mere functionary, teacher, or leader. Christians like to be in contact with their priests and to be visited and encouraged by them. They expect their priests to succeed in establishing a true family spirit among them, the visible expression of that mystical union that invisibly binds together the members of the Body of Christ. They want their pastor especially to be a faithful and living image of Jesus Christ.

When the priest lives up to the expectations of the faithful in the measure of the gifts he has received, it is then that, as a man of God, he realizes the human conditions for a fruitful apostolate. In that case his sheep will gladly agree that he follows and applies to himself the stern rule of conduct that St. Paul outlined for all those who, like young Timothy, would be commissioned to promote the kingdom of Christ crucified: "Preach the word, be urgent in season, out of season; reprove, entreat, rebuke with all patience and teaching. For there will come a time when they will not endure the sound doctrine: but having itching ears, will heap up to themselves teachers according to their own lusts, and they will turn away their hearing from the truth and turn aside rather to fables." [1]

The priest will have to be courageous in the accomplishment of his mission. "In season and out of season," he must bring to his human brethren the eternal and always efficacious word of God. He must not be timid in his expression; he must know nothing of the concessions and reticences of human pleading. As a minister of the Word, the conduct of the priest must not be that of the many who waters down the word of God. He must preach the word of God in its purity 'such as it came from God . . . in Jesus Christ,' " as Cardinal Suhard said.[2] He must not be stopped merely by the human fear of giving displeasure. When circumstances dictate that, objectively, the good of souls calls for words and attitudes that will not be popular—after prayer, reflection, and consultation—he must remember what St. Paul said: "For am I now seeking the favor of men, or of God? Or am I seeking to please men? If I were still trying to please men, I should not be a servant of Christ." [3]

The priest, of course, may never forget his sacred character and his spiritual authority. But he should also avoid any form of paternalism. His ideal must be to bring his charges to adulthood in the faith—to form Christian personalities that are well informed, competent in the religious field as well as in the secular, aware of their responsibility toward God, anxious to take an active part in the life of the Church, and of receiving the grace to put their talents at the service of Christ, who lives in His chosen People.

The minister of Christ should think of himself as one who has received the mission of sowing the faith. He should realize that he is entrusted with the cultivation of an enlight-

ened faith among Christians, of a faith that is
confident and strong enough to move moun-
tains. He should never forget the question put
to Christ: "When the Son of Man comes, will
He find, do you think, faith on the earth?" [5]

In this age of the triumph of science, tech-
nology, and free thought, he should not be
ashamed of the gospel.[6] He should not empty
the doctrine of Christ of its genuine content,
but he must proclaim it, supremely confident
in the knowledge that if he makes known the
gospel in all its purity and depth, his message
will prove to be the answer to the disquiet and
the thirst for truth which the Holy Spirit stirs
up so copiously in the soul of modern man.

The priest of Jesus is to be the minister of
hope. He betrays his mission if he does not
proclaim constantly and firmly that "here we
have no permanent city, but we seek for the
city that is to come." [7] He should see everything from the vantage point of eternity. He
should teach Christians to wait, in a life that
is temporary, for the coming of the Master,
and to consider the relative and unstable character of all human values: "For you were once
darkness, but now you are light in the Lord.
Walk, then, as children of light . . . testing
what is well pleasing to God; and have no
fellowship with the unfruitful works of dark-

ness, but rather expose them. . . Awake, sleeper, and arise from among the dead, and Christ will enlighten thee." [8]

The priest must be desirous to spread and to foster at every turn [9] the fire of charity that Christ has come to bring on earth.[10] At ordination he receives the liturgical chasuble from the hands of the bishop who says to him: "Receive the garment of the priest which signifies charity; for God is powerful enough to increase it in your soul and thus perfect His work." [11] From that moment the priest must draw profit from every contact to help the Christian People to be more deeply attached to God, and to develop his fraternal affection for all men.

Bishops and priests, then, are the sacred instruments Christ uses for the advance and transformation of His People as they make their way here below toward the House of the Father. They are the ambassadors Christ gave His Church that she may be able to be officially represented before God. In the exercise of their mission, bishops and priests are the external visible instruments used by Jesus to diffuse the Holy Spirit among His children. Let us look with the eyes of faith, then, on these ordained ministers. Let us see in them Jesus Himself.

II
Apostolic Work of Pastors

1. IN THE SERVICE OF CHRIST OFFERING SACRIFICE IN THE MIDST OF HIS PEOPLE

Through the ministerial priesthood Christ makes it possible for His people to have access to the sacramental offering of His redeeming sacrifice and the graces that flow therefrom.

The whole life of Jesus on earth was a constant immolation. Filled with the spirit of a redeemer, Jesus considered each occupation of the day as an act of obedience to the Father's will to save all men. He lived only to give glory to His Father and to save the world. But on closer inspection we see that these daily immolations only prepared and gradually made ready the great final immolation: the Victim that He was to offer one day on Calvary as the Supreme High Priest of the New Testament. "As soon as 'the word was made flesh' (John 1, 14), He showed Himself to the world in His priestly office by making an act of submission to the eternal Father which was to last all the days of His life: 'Coming into the world, He says: Behold I come . . . to do Thy will, O God' (Heb. 10, 5-7). He was destined to bring this act to full perfection in a marvelous manner in the bloody sacrifice of the Cross. 'It is in this "will" that we have been sanctified through the offering of the Body of Jesus Christ once for all' (Heb. 10, 10). His whole activity among men has no other intent." [1]

In the same way, in accordance with His example, the whole life of the People of God should be directed toward the Eucharistic sacrifice. The spiritual offerings of the interior priesthood, of which mention was made above, make up the human elements that we must prepare for the Mass, so that, under the symbols of bread and wine, these elements may be united to the body and blood of the only-begotten Son, our Lord Jesus Christ. They would not be an offering agreeable to the Father and accepted by Him, if they were not integrated with Jesus' sacrifice in the Mass.

But who is able to make the sacrifice of Christ mysteriously present on our altars and to make of it the sacrifice of the People of God? Those to whom the Lord said: "Do this in remembrance of Me"; [2] those who have received ordination to the priesthood from Christ through the Church. It is only in their hands, anointed with the sacred oils, that Jesus —through the bishop—has placed the chalice with wine and the paten with bread, saying: "Receive the power to offer sacrifice to God and to celebrate Mass both for the living and the dead. In the name of the Lord." Only ministerial priests are delegated by the High Priest to continue the mystery of the sacrifice of redemption in the midst of His holy People.

Christ willed, then, that His ministerial priests should be at the service of the People of God, ever ready to fulfill their sacred ministry in order that from the rising of the sun even to the going down, a clean oblation might be made to God.[3] The Master has said: "You know that those who are regarded as rulers among the Gentiles lord it over them, and their great men exercise authority over them. But it is not so among you. On the contrary, whoever wishes to become great shall be your servant; for the Son of Man also has not come to be served but to serve, and to give His life as a ransom for many." [4]

"To be a servant" does not mean that priests should be content to offer "their" Mass without striving to bring about the active participation of the community of the faithful.[5] With full respect for liberty of conscience, they should make every effort to lead the members of the People of God to understand how just and worthy, how reasonable and salutary it is to unite themselves to the sacrifice of the New Covenant. "Now when the faithful take part in the great liturgical action with so much piety and attention that it can be said of them 'whose faith and devotion are known to You, O Lord,' under such circumstances their faith cannot help but be stirred with a greater ardor prompted by charity; their piety cannot but grow strong and fervent. One and all, they will consecrate themselves to further the glory of God; and in their eager desire to be rendered similar to Jesus Christ who suffered such cruel torments, they will surely offer up themselves, with and through the Sovereign Priest, as a spiritual sacrifice." [6]

In offering the Eucharistic sacrifice, the priest must be aware that he stands at the altar as the representative of the whole People of God. The whole Church makes an offering through his holy ministry, as we read in the Canon of the Mass: "Thy ministers, as also Thy holy people, offer unto Thy supreme Majesty, of the gifts bestowed upon us, the pure Victim, the holy Victim, the all-perfect Victim; the holy Bread of eternal life and the chalice of everlasting salvation." However, as a mediator, the priest should not be content to celebrate the Eucharist acting as a mere intermediary or delegate; on the contrary, he must strive to make the faithful take the active part that is theirs in this act of worship.

"When the people make their offering along with the priest, the members of the Church do not fulfill the visible liturgical rite in the same manner as the priest himself; this is an office that belongs only to the minister delegated by God for that purpose. But they make the offering inasmuch as they unite their prayers of praise, impetration, expiation and thanksgiving to the prayers or mental intentions of the priest, and even of the Sovereign Priest, presenting these to God the Father with the very same exterior rite that the priest has offered up the Victim. . ." [7]

Christ also makes use of ministerial priests to apply the fruits of His sacrifice to those whom He wishes to save. This takes place through the sacraments. The sacraments are the channels through which the stream of graces that flow from His death and resurrection reach out to the souls of men.

Without Baptism, the rebirth of the sinner by water and the Holy Spirit, the Christian life and the Christian's share in the royal priesthood, could not even have a beginning. Without Confirmation these happy beginners would run the risk of never attaining to their spiritual maturity. Without the Eucharist, "the medicine of immortality and pledge of eternal life," there would be lacking the necessary sustenance for life and growth. Without Penance it would be impossible, after falling from grace, to be reborn. The development of the People of God is inconceivable, moreover, without the two sacraments of fecundity and multiplication, Holy Orders and Marriage. Finally, of what supreme advantage is Extreme Unction, accompanied by Holy Viaticum, for the strengthening of the sick and, in the case of the dying, to introduce them to the eternal temple of the risen Christ! The ministers of these sacraments are, so to speak, the arteries whereby the Head of the Mystical Body brings to His members the living forces that will guarantee their spiritual re-animation and their progressive sharing in divine Life.

The very existence and exercise of the royal priesthood by the faithful are therefore conditioned by sacramental union with Christ. The conclusion, therefore, is that the People of God have a right to the Mass and the sacraments. "Laymen have a right to receive from the clergy, in accordance with the rules of ecclesiastical discipline, the spiritual blessings and especially the helps necessary for salvation." [8] Consequently, those who have been ordained by Christ to be the purveyors of these blessings have an obligation to see to it that there is a yield from this sacred deposit. There is an imperative duty for them to be accessible and affable to those who call on their services: "Let a man so account us, as servants of Christ and stewards of the mysteries of God. Now here it is required in stewards that a man be found trustworthy." [9]

It would be wrong to consider, as some sort of clerical domination, the fact that the priest presides over the Eucharistic sacrifice or has a decisive voice in the distribution of the sacraments. One who understands that Christ makes the offering and distributes the sacraments will not see in the part of the priest anything but a mission that Christ has confided to him for the spiritual good of the People of God. It is precisely in order that this people may be what it is called to be—a priestly community a royal priesthood — that Jesus appeals to His priests to form them for this task, and to assist them in its realization. The sacred ministry is performed in obedience to Christ.

Consequently, it is wrong to say that according to Catholic doctrine the faithful cannot come into direct contact with God without the instrumentality of a priest. The priest is not the indispensable intermediary of grace. It is not a question of an approach in two stages, as if the Spirit had to pass from God to His people through the hands of a creature. The sole mediator of grace is Christ. When He makes use of a priest as an instrument to confer grace, this instrumentality cannot act as a screen to the principal cause, nor can it be conceived with respect to divine grace, as an intermediate stage. In the person of His minister, it is Christ Himself who directly touches the soul by means of His Spirit, and "while the sacraments of the Church are administered exteriorly, it is Christ Himself who brings about the effect in souls." [10] You who make such frequent contacts with your Master at Mass and the sacraments are familiar with this mysterious presence. Did you ever think that direct access to Him was barred to you, and that you had to pass through an intermediary? Your faith tells you, and religious experience proves it: "Neither he who plants is anything, nor he who waters, but God who gives the growth." [11]

2. IN THE SERVICE OF CHRIST TEACHING IN THE MIDST OF HIS PEOPLE

Through the authorized ministers of His Word, Christ makes it possible for His people, and gives them the right to attain revealed truth without fear of error, as it has been preserved in the Bible, apostolic tradition, and the teaching of the Church. This *Magisterium* is a living organism that has the assistance and the authority of Christ Himself.

Since you have the duty and the right to bear witness before the world, you should know, and must have it in your power to know, the doctrine of Christ. You must bear witness with complete objectivity and fidelity. The gospel of Jesus is a teaching that comes from God: "My teaching is not My own, but His who sent Me." [1] It is a sacred deposit. We pass it on to others, but we have no right to betray it, to abridge it, or to change it by one iota. St. Paul speaks of this most explicitly in his Epistle to the Galatians: "I marvel that you are so quickly deserting him who called you to the grace of Christ, changing to another gospel; which is not another gospel, except in this respect, that there are some who trouble you, and wish to pervert the gospel of Christ. But even if we or an angel from heaven should preach a gospel to you other than that which we have preached to you, let him be anathema." [2]

At this point a problem presents itself for the People of God. What should we do to remain faithful to the teaching revealed by Jesus if—while the truth must be one and the same —unanimity were to be lost with regard to what is true? Let us be reassured, for Christ has not left us orphans. He has promised us the assistance of a divine Advocate to safeguard truth. "If you love Me, keep My commandments. And I will ask the Father, and He will give you another Advocate to dwell with you forever, the Spirit of truth whom the world cannot receive, because it neither sees Him nor knows Him. But you shall know Him, because He will dwell with you, and be in you." [3]

Christ teaches in the midst of His people and by His people. He sends forth His Spirit constantly, and He will never allow His "teaching body" to lose one particle of His truth. His Holy Church will always remain one in the teaching of Jesus, because He Himself will bring it about that she be infallible in the interpretation of His gospel. In its totality the *Una Sancta* will always preserve the sacred deposit: "Preserve, says St. Paul, the deposit; keep inviolate and unspotted the 'talent' of the Catholic faith. What has been entrusted to you, that must remain with you, and must be handed on. If you have received gold, it must be gold that you pass on.[4] The Bible is the inspired source from which the Church extracts its doctrine; it is also the paternal mansion in which her sons may keep and find ever new the legacy of their common Father.[5] But individual Christians or groups of Christians may err. Where may the truth be found? The genuine interpretation of the teachings of Jesus may be found through apostolic tradition in accordance with the rule laid down by St. Vincent of Lérins: "In the Catholic Church we must strive with all our might to maintain *quod ubique, quod semper, et quod ab omnibus creditum est;* in other words, what has been everywhere believed, at all times, by all." [6]

In this area also, Jesus has promised to assist the Church. Catholic theology from age to age repeats that the faithful are guaranteed infallibility "in credendo." In other words, Christ gives His people the assurance that they will not err in those beliefs they unanimously consider as revealed truth. But those who make the act of faith also need some visible form of protection against error. In all things and at all times, Christ has shown Himself to be truly human. He always respects human and visible agents. Even in the sphere of fidelity to His doctrine, He wished to give His people guarantees of authenticity that can be grasped in human terms.

He proclaimed to the apostolic college, and, therefore, to the episcopal college—Pope and bishops—who are the extension of His teaching ministry, that He would be with them "all days, even unto the consummation of the world." [7] And the episcopal college, from the very beginning, has always been conscious of this promise. When bishops have gathered as a Council, they have always passed judgment as an organ possessing authority, sure of the truth of the sentence it pronounces; in other words, certain of its infallibility when it exercises its supreme authority in the field of revealed doctrine. The episcopal college possesses this prerogative not only when it meets in an Ecumenical Council, but also when, though scattered throughout various Churches, it governs, it expresses itself with the same unanimity and in the form used in such final judgments." [8]

Furthermore, the Lord addressed Himself to Peter in person and, as the context of His promise suggests, to all the successors of Peter. He gave them the assurance that in their mission and in their function as pastors of the episcopal body, they would receive special di-

vine aid to safeguard them against error,
whenever they exercise the supreme function
of an *ex cathedra* definition.

Christ has founded His Church upon Peter,
and it is Peter He makes use of, in order to
preserve among His people His words, which
are spirit and life. St. Ambrose speaks of this
in the following terms: "It is to Peter that He
said: 'Thou art Peter, and upon this rock I
will build My Church.' Where Peter is, then,
there is the Church; where the Church is,
there is no death but eternal life." [9] If, when
speaking as head of the Church, in the field of
faith and morals, Peter and his successors are
infallible, this does not mean that they have
the right to add anything to the truths con-
tained in the Bible and the tradition of the
People of God. The assistance of the Holy
Spirit has been guaranteed to them only inso-
far as, after prayer, consultation and deep
study, they declare, acting in the plenitude of
their power, that such and such a point of doctrine has been revealed.

The Catholic hierarchy, inasmuch as it is
the teaching body of the Church, teaches the
gospel of Christ infallibly. However, the
teaching body did not receive from the beginning a perfectly explicit expression of Catholic
truths which it gradually presents to the Peo-

ple of God. In the Church there is a certain
development of doctrine. How does the message undergo this process of development? Is
it solely by the action of the Holy Spirit on the
episcopacy that this deeper insight into the
gospel is acquired? No, the whole Church,
bishops and faithful, are in a certain sense involved in this growth in the understanding of
the Word. The whole Church under the guid-
ance of the Holy Spirit gives infallible witness
to divine revelation. To come to the full
knowledge of revealed doctrine, the teaching
body does not rely exclusively on the Holy
Spirit's action on the bishops; it listens also to
the action of the same spirit at work in the
People of God. Thus, the teaching body not
only speaks to the People of God, it also listens to this People in whom Christ continues
His teaching.[10]

Besides these extraordinary pronounce-
ments of the teaching Church, there is also the
day-to-day teachings that Jesus gives to His
chosen People through the hierarchy. Theirs
is the "daily pressing anxiety," [11] lest the *Una
Sancta* deviate from the *verba vitae,* the words
of life. Jesus says to Popes and bishops: "He
who hears you, hears Me; and he who rejects
you, rejects Me; and he who rejects Me, rejects Him who sent Me." [12] And so the teach-

ing body of the Church must consider itself as commissioned by Christ in the service of the truth: "For God was truly in Christ, recon· ciling the world to Himself by not reckoning against men their sins and by entrusting to us the message of reconciliation. On behalf of Christ, therefore, we are acting as ambassadors, God, as it were, appealing through us." [13]

The Bible, Tradition, and the Teaching of the Pope and bishops should be the inspiration of your witness, that it may be in accord with the truths that Christ wishes to teach through you. He does not leave you to your own resources, as we said, but He offers you both His invisible and visible assistance. Your pastors, far from guiding you according to their fancy, in God's name fulfill the part of "oracle," authorized and necessary. Jesus has put them at your service that you may have sufficient knowledge of the message. It is your mission to pass it on to your brethren in the faith and to all the others — how many of them!—who are still awaited in the Father's house.

Be eager, therefore, to seek assistance from those who are your fathers in the faith. Insist on help from them. In this manner, let your religious attitude be that of adults in the faith.

Be fully aware of your responsibilities and apply yourselves to study, meditation and prayer, so as to acquire, under the direction of the Church's teaching body, a genuine competence in the doctrine of Christ.

3. IN THE SERVICE OF CHRIST RULING IN THE
MIDST OF HIS PEOPLE

(a) *The Christian before the World*

In the person of the members of the clergy, Christ the King wishes to guarantee to the faithful His light and His encouragement for the accomplishment in justice and in charity, of the work of humanizing, spiritualizing, and consecrating the world— in view of its final destiny.

The People of God are entrusted with the particular and irreplaceable mission of making the world more human, of helping to diffuse the spiritual element in it, and of orienting it toward God. But this mission has to be fulfilled in the midst of a thoroughly secular existence. Every Christian has been assigned a definite place by Providence. If he does not accomplish his task, if he does not show the necessary zeal, nobody else can do so in his place. It is obvious that neither priests nor ecclesiastical authority as such have direct charge of this consecration of the world.[1]

Does this mean that schools and laboratories, offices and factories, shops and farms, places of recreation and popular assembly, must be shut off to priestly influence? You who want to cooperate with your bishop do not share this opinion, for you are anxious to have ecclesiastical authority help you in the fulfillment of your mission on earth. This is also the case with your professional and social groups, both of which would like to have "an ecclesiastical assistant." Naturally, you do not expect the priest to give you orders about the execution of these secular tasks. The priest cannot claim rights and responsibilities in these areas, when neither religion nor morals are involved. What you do expect from your pastors is to be able to receive from them authoritative judgments, counsel and encouragement, with regard to your mission on earth.

Pius XII said, "The materialism and atheism of a world in which millions of Christians are forced to live in isolation, helps to form them into complete personalities. Otherwise, how will they be able to resist being overcome by the masses that surround them? What holds good for everybody is especially true of the lay apostle who has not only to defend himself, but also to make conquests." [2]

Your spiritual offerings will not be pleasing

to the Father and your witness will have a hollow ring about it, if your conduct in the midst of the world is not in conformity with the teaching of Christ, and respectful of the rights of others. The mentality of the modern world and the atmosphere in which you have to spend your life are hardly favorable to thoroughly Christian attitudes. There is considerable confusion at the present moment, and one would think that Satan is applying himself to the systematic corruption of the truth." [3]

For this reason, you desire, quite rightly, the assistance of the clergy in acquiring a Christian outlook and a Christian approach to the demands of your secular calling. You wish to reflect and pray with them in order to understand how natural law and the doctrine of the Church on the family and society may be applied to the concrete situations in which Providence has placed you. Seek to be instructed in the works of those theologians who have the approval of the Church. Listen with respectful attention to the teaching of your pastors, as well as preachers and chaplains to whom the bishops have entrusted the mission of being the living echo of Christ's doctrine. May they consider it their primary obligation to foster lay vocations and to help you form a truly adult, Christian conscience.

Let this be your conviction, that when you listen to the teaching voice of the Church, you are listening to Christ Himself; not only when the Church speaks approvingly, but every bit as much when its apostolic duty compels it to declare that such and such an attitude or this and that decision is not in conformity with the requirements of the will of our Savior.

It is the mission of sacred ministers to lend support and encouragement to the People of God. It is not easy to be faithful to Christian principles in the struggle for existence, even when the path to be followed is clearly discerned. The spirit of gain, egoism, and sloth are evil tendencies every man feels in himself; they are a threat to every Christian conscience. Furthermore, those who wish to be faithful to Christ in the midst of the world are, and always will be, the butt of opposition, criticism, and persecution. Have no illusions about it, for Christ predicted it: "If you were of the world, the world would love what is its own. But because you are not of the world, but I have chosen you out of the world, therefore the world hates you." [4]

Because of such difficulties, the Christian desires the presence and encouragement of a man of God. As you know by experience, Christ makes use of him to give you a perceptible sign of His friendship and support. Those who have no contact with a priest have no idea what the visit of a priest or a conversation with him can do in the struggle for existence, or in time of trial. The minister of religion is, so to speak, a living sacrament and a living word. Through him Christ is visibly present in human form among those who struggle together with Him for the consecration of the world.

(b) *The Lay Apostolate*

By means of the pastors of His People, Christ calls on some of the faithful either to lend their help to the clergy in carrying out their mission, or else to accept a mandate for the systematic promotion of the apostolate that is proper to the layman within the sphere of Catholic Action.

By virtue of Baptism and Confirmation, all members of the People of God have a right to the assistance of the Holy Spirit, and Jesus the Priest, wishes to continue His saving action through them. Accordingly, pastors may make a special appeal to some laymen to help them put into effect their methodical efforts for the spread and defense of the kingdom of Christ. No difficulty is presented by this call of Jesus that asks them, through the voice of ecclesiastical authorities, to help Him in a more systematic manner and within a specified area.

Thus, the hierarchy places the care of opening and directing Christian schools or charitable institutions in the hands of certain groups of the faithful. In the same manner, Christian men or women may be asked by the bishop to teach religion in a State-owned or public school. Some may take up the task of preparing women for their role as Christian mothers, or children for Confirmation or first Holy Communion—these will be the zealous promoters of useful activities, taking on the responsibility of parish movements and other similar works. In all these various types of co-operation, they will freely give of their time, either all or part, so as to help put into operation amidst the People of God, activities whose direction and, in part, execution, are in the hands of the Pope, the bishops or members of the clergy. In all these areas, therefore, it is a question of aiding the hierarchy in a sector of the apostolate that is their direct responsibility.

However, in the vast field of the apostolate there are areas, as we mentioned above, wherein the hierarchy is not directly involved, and which pertain directly to the laity. We are here speaking of secular life, both public and private. By means of the faithful, Christ introduces into this sphere Christian principles, a Christian atmosphere, a Christian way of making use of temporal goods and means. This is the vocation and the specific mission of the faithful who live in such surroundings. But how will they acquit themselves of this task? Will they fulfill it as it should be fulfilled? In other words, will they be sufficiently able, enterprising, persevering, and will they follow methods that are in conformity with the spirit of the gospel? Will the results they achieve be adequate? The pastors of the People of God cannot be indifferent to all these problems.

In the final analysis, pastors must look and see whether in the midst of the People of God the members measure up to the expectations of Christ. Jesus said to Peter: "Confirma fratres tuos"—strengthen thy brethren.[1] He gave an imperative mission to the whole apostolic college: "Go, therefore, and make disciples of all nations, baptizing them in the name of the Father, and of the Son, and of the Holy Spirit, teaching them to observe all that I have commanded you."[2]

Jesus wishes to make use of the organization of the Church so as to ensure that everybody does his duty, that his members perform their tasks perfectly. Consequently, pastors, who are preoccupied with the climate that prevails in our modern world, and realizing the unique part that laymen can play in the sanctification of the profane have addressed themselves to the more generous among the faithful, saying: "organize yourselves and help one another so that a growing number of Christians may become aware of the demands of their priestly role. You yourselves must become responsible apostles wherever you live." The answer to this invitation of the hierarchy is Catholic Action.

Catholic Action is a collective and organized apostolate of the People of God, directed by laymen themselves who have received a special and direct mandate from the hierarchy, and having as its objective to help the Christian people measure up to their mission to be, in union with Jesus, priest, witness, and consecrator of their earthly surroundings.

Such Catholic Action can take on various forms. At times, it will lay stress, for example on the apostolate among different social groups (specialized Catholic Action); at other times, it will especially direct its activities toward the environment of the home (Catholic Action of a general character); then again it may concern itself more directly with particularly urgent situations ("shock" Catholic Action). In all instances it will be the action of Christians who have understood that the kingdom of Christ will not come on earth and society will not become Christian unless dedicated laymen help one another to act like Christians worthy of the name, making their Christianity incarnate and rendering the general atmosphere more favorable to the requirements of the life of Christ among His People.

These three forms of Catholic Action should complete each other, for at present all three of them are becoming more and more indispensable. Without specialized Catholic Action, what will become of the various social groups? How will it be possible to teach and train Christians to adopt a truly Christian attitude in the complex problems posed by the faith, when confronted by the realities of this world? Who will concern himself with bringing Christian principles to bear on ideological movements, or on national and international institutions? Without Catholic Action of a general character, what would become of the unity that ought to reign in the Body of Christ? Who will apply himself to the development and organization of that visible brotherhood that should exist among all the inhabitants of a district, a parish, a diocese, the

Church, all mankind? If there were no Catholic Action "shock" groups who would witness to the truth and goodness of Christ among those individuals, families, and neighborhoods, where the process of de-Christianization and de-humanization is so deeply rooted that, besides the other forms of apostolate extraordinary and specially adapted efforts are needed?

You, both men and women, who often meet in some branch of Catholic Action, are all members of one single army of peace. You are organized in such a way that your general Catholic Action operations are, in fact, the indispensable complement of your specialized efforts on the parochial and diocesan levels. and you call on "shock" Catholic Action whenever such an operation is demanded for effective results. It is likewise clear that general activities and urgent specialized intervention will only have a temporary and superficial effect if the formation of "shock" groups and their assault are not previously asserted on the social level.[3]

Continue living and working in close fraternal understanding. All of you have the same objective. You all have the obligation to fulfill the hope that Christ and His Church place in your organization and in its members. May it come about, through your work, that the faithful fully occupied in secular life, may be more and more united with Jesus who offers sacrifice, teaches, and exercises this rule in the royal priesthood of His chosen People. Thus, you will continue to be the joy and honor of the Church and the glory of Christ: "Omnia in gloriam Dei facite" Do all for the glory of God.[4]

There are many occasions for contacts between laymen and ordained ministers in the field of the systematically organized apostolate. Lay participation in carrying out tasks which does not involve the direct responsibility of the hierarchy, calls on both sides for a clearer perception of their respective functions, and a genuine, deep esteem for the different missions that Jesus has entrusted to both.

Lay apostles, more than others, should honor and love the Sovereign Pontiff, the visible representative of the Supreme Pastor. The power to open wide the pastures of truth and divine grace to the whole universe, as well as to welcome, help, and defend the sheep and lambs of the fold, has been entrusted to him. They must be solidly one with their bishop and with the episcopate of their country, sharing their efforts to create a true community spirit, and to spread on all levels of society the desire, as Christians, to be present, to witness, and to penetrate into every sphere of society.

Militant members of Catholic Action, both men and women, should strive to see Christ in everyone of His ordained ministers, fostering in themselves as well as developing in persons around them, a lively faith in the divine character of his mission. They should compare their observations and experiences. They should meditate and pray together, never failing to approach problems from a religious point of view, and to adopt an openly supernatural attitude in the search for solutions.

For their part, ordained ministers must have trust in the action of Christ in the souls of their lay collaborators; they must bear in mind their abilities and the graces that they receive. They must not prevent laymen from assuming the responsibilities that belong to them, out of a desire to do everything themselves, without allowing them, in their impatience, to acquire the experience that the actual exercise of the apostolate should give them. The diffusion of the Christian ideal that laymen can bring about in the very midst of secular surroundings is an indispensable apostolic factor in the full development of the divine life that Christ desires. Their contribution is a unique one. The ceaseless concern and the genuine preoccupation of an ordained minister must be to encourage this force and to urge it to reach maturity. He must help it achieve its fullest effectiveness by a strong organization on the diocesan, national, and international levels. Christian laymen must also organize themselves systematically for the defense and triumph of Christian principles at the very core of the powerful international organizations, whose influence is becoming more and more decisive for the life of humanity.[5]

CONCLUSION
One Priest: Christ Jesus

The imposition of hands is the rite whereby Christ communicates His priesthood to bishops, to priests, and to the baptized. By this sacramental action, He institutes in His Church and in the world a community of Christians qualified to continue His work of sanctification, of witness and consecration of the world.

From the beginning of Christianity the People of God have always attached considerable importance to the mysterious rite of the imposition of hands. The first apostles used it in communicating to others the Holy Spirit whom they themselves had received. Since that time the Church has constantly assisted with deep emotion at the performance of this sacred action.

At the consecration of a bishop, the bishop-elect, surrounded by relatives and brothers in the faith, presents himself before the three consecrating bishops.

Before admitting him to the apostolic college, the three bishops, as a preliminary step, make certain of the candidate's union with the Church of which Christ is the soul. First of all they take up the reading of the bulls of the successor of Peter—the Pope of Rome—authorizing the new bishop to receive the fullness of the priesthood, and indicating what part of the fold will be entrusted to his care. Next he is questioned on the orthodoxy of his faith, and his desire to remain faithful to the *una, sancta, catholica et apostolica Ecclesia* (one, holy, Catholic and apostolic Church). Assured in this way, of the legitimacy of the consecration, the three consecrating bishops then confer on him a total and plenary union in the priesthood of Christ.

They devoutly put their hands on his head and say: "Receive the Holy Spirit"; then, raising their voices in earnest prayer, they beseech the Lord to confer on this priest the sacrament of the fullness of the priesthood: *Comple in sacerdote tuo ministerii tui summam, et ornamentis totius glorificationis instructum, caelestis unguenti rore sanctifica*—fulfill in Your priest the perfection of Your work, and having clothed him with all the ornaments of Your glory, sanctify him with the dew of heavenly ointment." This simple action and the words of the ritual are enough. The priest has become a bishop. After twenty centuries there has been realized in him the grace which St.

Paul, speaking to young bishop Timothy, was referring to: "Do not neglect the grace that is in thee, granted to thee by reason of prophecy with the laying on of hands of the presbyterat." [1] There we have the essence of the sacrament.[2]

Everything that follows in the solemn ceremony of an episcopal consecration gravitates about this center, and its only purpose is to underscore its sublimity and importance. The sacred oil with which his head and hands are anointed signify that he has become a high priest, prophet and king of the People of God. The symbol of his powers is placed in his hands: the crozier of a pastor and the ring that binds him to his Church. Finally, the three consecrating bishops put in his hand the book of the Gospels and say to him: "*Accipe Evangelium, et vade, praedica populo tibi commisso* — receive the gospel, go and announce it to the people entrusted to you."

In union with the bishop of Rome, the successor of Peter, the other bishops are the proper pastors of the People of God. Each bishop has the ordinary responsibility of the flock entrusted to him. However, it is his privilege, as was shown above, to call upon others for aid. It is in his power to communicate sacramentally a real but limited sharing in that priesthood of Christ which the imposition of hands imparted to him in all its fullness.

The ceremony of ordination is very much like the consecration of a bishop.

The candidate presents himself before those who have already received the power of Orders: the bishop and his priests. Since he is destined to serve the local Church they do not wish to put him at the helm of the ship without consulting the passengers, for as the bishop says: "Our fathers have wisely set down that the faithful should be consulted about the suitability of the candidate chosen to be placed in charge of the service of the altar." When the people have given their consent, the bishop explains to the ordained, for one last time, the tasks that will be entrusted to him, namely, to make offering at the altar, to bless, to preside, to preach, and to baptize.

When all those present have prayed God and all His saints to grant His servant "the blessing of the Holy Spirit and the power of priestly grace," the bishop stands before the altar of the Lord and the priests form a circle about him. In the midst of a solemn silence, the bishop places his hands on the young levite and the priests each in turn do likewise.

Then takes place the solemn Eucharistic prayer in which the bishop, in the name of the

Church, addresses the Father Almighty: *Da, quaesumus, omnipotens Pater, in hunc famulum tuum Presbyterii dignitatem; innova in visceribus eius spiritum sanctitatis; ut acceptum a te, Deus, secundi meriti munus accipiat, censuramque morum exemplo suae conversationis insinuet* — We beseech You, almighty Father, give Your servant the dignity of the priesthood; renew in his heart the spirit of holiness in order that he may obtain from You the office that is second in dignity, and that he may cause virtue to be loved by the example of his conduct."

After these essential rites, visible signs will, in this case also, outwardly represent what the Holy Spirit has brought about in the soul of the new priest. The bishop clothes him with a stole—the sweet yoke of the Lord; then the chasuble—the priestly garment that signifies the charity he must put on in all his actions. The consecrating bishop prays out loud that the priest may always take to heart the teaching of the Church and the direction of the faithful who are entrusted to his care: "Bring it about that by meditating night and day on Your holy law they may believe what they have read, teach what they believe, and practice what they teach. . . . That they may give good example and add preaching to this."

All priests, the very old as well as the very young, retain poignant memories of this ceremony, the turning-point of their lives, when they felt the hands of the bishop pressing down on their heads and the sacramental words binding them to Christ the Priest irrevocably. They are thus the friends of the Master. By the same token, they are bound to help Him carry His Cross, and to make His plans and His apostolic enterprises their own. They have categorically given themselves to Christ and to the souls whose sanctification it will be their duty to assure.

Among the People of God there is yet another form of consecration. It is less spectacular, but every bit as real: Confirmation. No one is consecrated or ordained without previously receiving this sacrament which, continuing the effects of Baptism, communicates to those reborn in the waters of salvation the quality of Christians who have come of age and are committed to living the faith. It is a question here of "a spiritual power that makes one fit for certain religious acts." [3]

Even in Baptism, the basic essential rite of ablution that purifies the soul and incorporates it in Christ is preceded by a twofold imposition of hands by the minister on the head of the candidate, as a sign of God's protection against the devil, and of the graces that are to come into his heart from God's paternal hand. However, only in Confirmation is the imposition of hands a sacramental sign.

In Confirmation the sacred rites have the same characteristic notes as in the sacrament of Holy Orders.

Young people who have been baptized present themselves before the bishop. As they kneel before him he imposes hands on all of them, and asks that the seven gifts of the Holy Spirit come down to them. Then follows the supreme moment of this ceremony. Each one of those to be confirmed comes up to the bishop, who lays his hands upon them and pronounces the words of Confirmation: "I sign you with the sign of the Cross, and I anoint you with the chrism of salvation in the name of the Father and of the Son and of the Holy Spirit. Peace be with you." And that is the essence of the ceremony.

While the sacrament of the Holy Spirit is conferred by this action, further rites serve to make explicit the meaning of what has just taken place: the anointing with Holy Chrism, the royal sign of the holy cross on the candidate's forehead, the reference to the work of salvation and the strength received to cooperate in it—all this shows that by this sacrament one becomes an adult Christian, and is more intimately united with Christ, Priest, Prophet, and King of the People of God.

You can see, then, that the imposition of hands, accompanied by the sacramental words, is the often repeated rite that consecrates bishops, priests and those who are confirmed. These are the human actions that transmit the power merited for His Church by the Master. This is the manner in which He makes of His people a community of Christians able to continue His work of sanctification, witness, and consecration of the world. "But we have gifts differing according to the grace that has been given us." [4] However different our participation in the same gifts, it is obvious that our qualities must be harmoniously integrated in the general plan laid down by the Father.

Actually there is only one Christ and one priesthood. Sent as He was by the Father, and ordained in the sanctuary of the Virgin Mary by the Power of the Holy Spirit, Jesus is essentially a Priest. "Christ did not merely fill the function of priest; He is essentially such. Christ and priest are two interchangeable terms. From the first this priesthood is complete and perfect; and nobody can add anything to it." [5] By nature Christ is the Intermediary, the Mediator. He alone among men is worthy to approach the Father. He is the only One who wholly possesses the capacity to offer a victim that is acceptable, and to bring it about that there descends on men the fruits of truth and of grace.

Now the risen and glorious Christ continues His work. He has passed on His mission of representation and oblation to the Pope, and to those whom He has consecrated bishops and priests. He has given them a sacred trust. He has entrusted them with a holy ministry, a sacred service. Though members of the Body of Christ in their private lives, priests fulfill the role of organs of this Body every time it is Jesus' will to make use of them for the defense of the Church and to enhance her beauty. The Church is their *raison d'être*.

Let the consecrated ministers then love the People of God. Let them devote themselves, body and soul, to their advancement. Only by placing themselves humbly at the service of the Catholic Church will they meet the expectations of the Master and attain to the goal of their sublime vocation.

However, in the final analysis, the work of salvation concerns the People of God. The Supreme Pontiff offers to his Father an acceptable worship in His Church, through the royal priesthood of His People. The Incarnate Word constantly sends forth His message through His People. Finally, this royal priesthood is the instrument of Christ the King for the orientation of all creation toward God. It is the People of God who must attain to the fullness of Christ.

May the members of this priestly People be fully aware that they are called upon to sacrifice themselves for the glory of God. May they live in close union with Jesus and their pastors, in order that they may make of their whole life a holy oblation, a ceaseless work for the diffusion on earth of the Kingdom of God that will constitute the dawn of the Great Day.

At the Parousia, when God becomes All in All, it is this People of God that will be gloriously united to the Lamb forever. And then before the heavenly altar of the Lamb, the new canticle will be sung: "Worthy art Thou to take the scroll and to open its seals; for Thou wast slain, and hast redeemed us for God with Thy blood, out of every tribe, and tongue and people and nation, and hast made them for our God a kingdom and priests, and they shall reign over the earth." [6]

Issued at Bruges, on the Feast of St. Mark, April 25, 1961.

EMILE-JOSEPH
Bishop of Bruges

Notes and References

Foreword

1. Throughout this book the word "faithful" designates all those who have received in baptism the dignity of member of the Church. So the "faithful" are not only the laity but also religious, priests, bishops and the Pope. "Faithful" and "laity," then, are not interchangeable terms. When there is mention of the "People of God" this refers to the community composed of all those baptized, of all the faithful.

BIBLIOGRAPHY: Y. Congar-F. Varillon, *Sacerdoce et laïcat dans l'Eglise*, Paris, 1947; Y. Congar, *Jalons pour une théologie du laïcat*, Paris, 1953; J. Lecuyer, *Le sacerdoce dans le mystère du Christ*, Paris, 1957; G. Philips, *Le laïcat dans le mystère de l'Eglise*, in *La Revue nouvelle* 16 (1952), p. 538-49; K. Rahner, *L'Apostolat des laïcs*, in *Nouvelle Revue Théologique* 88 (1956), p. 3-33; L. Suenens, *Théologie de l'apostolat*, Bruges, 1951; E. C. Suhard, Cardinal, *Le Pretre dans la Cité*, in *D.C.* 46, (1949), col. 583-621, 769-814; G. Thils, *Mission du clergé et du laïcat*, Bruges, 1945; S. Tromp, *Corpus Christi quod est Ecclesia*, I: *Introductio generalis*, Romae, 1946; II: *De Christo capite*, Romae, 1960; III: *De Spiritu Christi Anima*, Rome, 1960.

2. *See* the bibliography of Pontifical documents and their commentaries in Università Cattolica del

Sacro Cuore—Milan, *L'Apostolato dei laici*, Bibliografia Sistematica, Milan, 1957, p. 1-9. Especially: Pius XI, Encyclical *Ubi Arcano*, in *A.A.S.* 14 (1922), p. 673-700; Pius XII, Allocution *De quelle consolation* to the members of the "First World Congress on the Apostolate of the Laity" (October 14, 1951), in *A.A.S.* 43 (1951), p. 786-92. *D.C.* 48 (1951), col. 1497-1504; Pius XII, Allocution *Six ans se sont écoulés* to the "Second World Congress of the Apostolate of the Laity" (October 5, 1957) in *A.A.S.* 49 (1957), p. 922-39, *D.C.* 54 (1957) col. 1413-1427; John XXIII, Encyclical *Ad Petri Cathedram* (June 29, 1959), in *A.A.S.* 51 (1959), p. 497-531, *D.C.* 56 (1959), col. 897-922; John XXIII, *Allocution to the Roman Delegates of Catholic Action* (January 10, 1960), in *A.A.S.* 52 (1960), p. 83-90, *D.C.* 57 (1960) col. 129-125.

3. Isaia 62, 10.

4. *See* Ephes. 3, 9. — E. Schillebeeckx, *Le Christ, Sacrement de la Rencontre de Dieu*, Paris, 1960.

5. *See* the bibliography in Università Cattolica—Milan, *op. cit.;* J. Hamer, *Bulletin d'ecclésiologie*, in *Revue Phil. et Théol.* 43 (1959), p. 325-62; G. Philips, *Etudes sur l'Apostolat des Laïcs*, in *Ephem. Theol. Lovanienses* 35 (1959), p. 877-903.

6. Among others: the two World Congresses on the Apostolate of the Laity held in Rome in 1951 and 1957.

7. *See* especially our Pastoral Letter of February 16, 1957, *Apostles of Jesus Christ*, in *Collectio Epistolarum Pastoralium*, Vol. XXVII, p. 13-22, Bruges, 1957.

8. *Osservatore Romano*, August 10, 1959.

Part One

The Royal Priesthood of all the Faithful

Chapter I

Nature of the Priesthood of All the Faithful

1. John, 1, 43.

2. John 18, 37.

3. Exod. 19, 5-6.

4. Isaia, 61, 6.

5. I Peter 2, 4-5.9. *See* B. Botte, A. Charlier, A. Robeyns, and B. Capelle, *Le sacerdoce des fidèles,* Louvain, 1935; L. Cerfaux, *Regale sacerdotium,* in *Revue des Sc. Phil. et Théol.* 28 (1939), p. 5-39, or else *Recueil Cerfaux,* Vol. 2, p. 283-315; P. Dabin, *Le sacerdoce royal des fidèles,* I: *Dans les livres saints;* II: *Dans la tradition ancienne et moderne,* Bruges 1941 and 1950; G. Thils, *Le pouvoir cultuel du baptisé* in *Ephem. Theol. Lovanienses* 15 (1938) R. 683-98; J. J. Weber, *Brèves Etudes Eucharistiques,* Paris, 1961, p. 163-69.

6. This capacity of offering a genuine spiritual sacrifice finds its completion in the mission of offering the Eucharistic sacrifice which Christ has given to the whole Christian People, as will be set forth in the second portion of this Pastoral Letter.

7. I Cor. 3, 9.

8. Ephes. 4, 7. 11-13. 16.

9. St. Augustine, *De Civitate Dei,* XX, 10; *M.L.* 41, 676.

Chapter II

The Priestly Work of the Faithful

1. LIFE IN UNION WITH CHRIST OFFERING SACRIFICE
IN THE MIDST OF HIS PEOPLE

1. Ephes. 1, 3-7.
2. Ps. 104, 1-5.
3. Matt. 6, 9-10.
4. John 1, 29.
5. Matt. 20, 12.
6. Col. I, 24-29.
7. Rom. 12, 1-2.
8. *See* J. Lecuyer, *Le sacerdoce dans le mystère du Christ,* Paris, 1957, p. 171-97.
9. Rom. 8, 26.
10. Apoc. 3, 11-13.

2. LIFE IN UNION WITH CHRIST, TEACHING IN THE
MIDST OF HIS PEOPLE

(a) *Christian Witness*

1. Rom. 1, 9.
2. Rom. 8, 29.
3. Ephes. 4, 15. —*See* the Radio Message of His Holiness John XXIII, Christmas 1960 (December 22, 1960), *Truth and Peace,* in *A.A.S.* 53 (1961) p. 5-15, *D.C.* 58 (1961), col. 65-74; Cardinal E. J. Van Roey, *Nos devoirs envers la vérité* (January 30, 1961) in *Lettres Pastorales,* Vol. 8, p. 603-06. *See,* also John 4, 23-24.
4. Rom. 1, 12.
5. "Witness in word and deed is the essential mission and responsibility of every Christian and of every Church" (*Ecumenical Review,* October 1960, p. 81).
6. Matt. 5, 14-16.

(b) *Apostolic Mission of the People of God.*

1. Rom. 10, 14.

2. 1 Peter 2, 9.

3. Matt. 4, 19.

4. "As for the Church, she has a triple mission to accomplish with regard to all: to make fervent believers able to cope with the requirements of the present age; to bring into the warm and salvific intimacy of the household those who are lingering at the threshhold; to bring back those who have wandered away from religion, whom she cannot abandon to their sad lot" (Pius XII, Allocution *De quelle consolation,* in *A.A.S.* 43 [1951] p. 788, *D.C.* 48 [1951] col. 1499).

5. 2 Cor. 11, 28-29.

6. 2 Cor. 5, 20.

7. 1 Cor. 2, 1-5.

8. 1 Cor. 13, 1.

(c) *Christian Tolerance*

1. On the problem of tolerance *see* Pius XII, Allocution *Ci riesce* to Italian Catholic jurists (December 6, 1953), in *A.A.S.* 45 (1953), p. 794-802, *D.C.* 50 (1953), col. 1601-1608; Cardinal J. Lercaro, Address *Tolérance et intolérance religieuse,* in *D.C.* 56 (1959), col. 335-348; R. Aubert, among other works, *Tolérance et communauté humaine*: Chrétiens dans un monde divisé, Tournai-Paris 1951; J. Lecler, *Histoire de la tolérance au siècle de la Réforme,* Paris, 1953; A. Léonard, *Dialogue des chrétiens et des non-chrétiens* in *Etudes religieuses,* 758, Brussels, 1959; A. Hartmann, *Vrai et fausse tolérance,* Paris, 1958.

2. Matt. 5, 44-48.

3. LIFE IN UNION WITH CHRIST, RULING IN THE MIDST OF HIS PEOPLE

(a) *The Kingship of Christ*

1. Ephes. 1, 10.

2. Rom. 8, 12-17.

(b) *A Royal People*

1. J. Lecuyer, *op. cit.*, p. 212-15.

2. E.-J. De Smedt, *Le Christ dans le quartier,* Bruges, 1960.

3. Matt. 10, 34.

4. Gen. 1, 26.

5. Gen. 1, 28.

6. Gen. 2, 5 and 15.

7. 1 Cor. 3, 9.

8. 1 Cor. 10, 31.

9. John 14, 34-35.

10. Matt. 25, 31-46.

11. *Didache*, 12, 3-5.

12. *See* John XXIII, Allocution *C'est bien volontiers,* on the high social value of electronic devices (March 18, 1961): "We have here an application of technical progress for the service of humanity, a use of machines to the advantage of spiritual values, a new and striking example of the mastery of mind over matter, and the fulfillment of the command given by the Creator to our first parents 'Fill the earth and subdue it' (Gen. 1, 28)" (*Osservatore Romano,* March 19, 1961).

13. Rom. 8, 22-24.

14. 1 Cor. 15, 28.

Chapter III

Religious and Members of Secular Institutes

1. Ephes. 5, 25-27.

2. S. Thomp, *Actio Catholica in Corpore Christi*, Romae, 1936, p. 10-16.

3. J. Hamer, *Place des religieux dans l'apostolat de l'Eglise*, in *Nouvelle Revue Théologique* 81 (1959), p. 271-81.

4. B. M. Chevignard, *Le rôle du prêtre dans l'éveil des vocations*, Paris, 1958, p. 36.

5. Matt. 16, 24-25.

6. Pius XII, Apostolic Constitution *Sponsa Christi* in *A.A.S.* 43 (1951), p. 14.

7. Heb. 13, 13-15.

8. Apoc. 14, 1-4.

Part Two

The People of God and Their Pastors

Chapter I

The Priestly Ministry

1. POPE AND BISHOPS

1. Matt. 28, 19-20.

2. Matt. 18, 18.

3. Matt. 16, 18-19.

4. John 21, 17.

5. Luke 22, 32.—*See* the two Allocutions of Pius XII to the cardinals and bishops present in Rome for the canonization of St. Pius X (May 31, 1954) and for the solemn proclamation of the liturgical feast of the Mother of God, Queen of heaven and

earth (November 2, 1954). In the first Allocution, *Si diligis . . . pasce* (*A.A.S.* 46 [1954], p. 313-17), Pius XII takes as his subject the teaching power of the hierarchy, and in the second *Magnificate Dominum*, its priestly and juridical power (*A.A.S.* 46 [1954], p. 666-77; *D.C.* 51 [1954], col. 705-710, 1427-1438).

6. 2 Thess. 3, 1.

7. Col. 1, 10.

8. *See* the Radio Address of John XXIII, Christmas 1960, *Vérité et Paix* and Cardinal E. J. Van Roey's Pastoral Letter, *Nos devoirs envers la verité* (January 30, 1961). *See* above, note 3 under *Christian Witness*.

2. PRIESTS

1. 2 Tim. 4, 2-4.—*See* Cardinal E. C. Suhard, *Le prêtre dans la cité, loc. cit.*, p. 601; A. M. Charue, *Le clergé diocésain tel qu'um évêque le voit et le souhaite*, Tournai, 1960.

2. Cardinal E. C. Suhard, *ibid.*, p. 207—2 Cor. 2, 17.

3. Gal. 1, 10.

4. A. Liégé, *Adultes dans le Christ*, in *Etudes religieuses* 735, Bruxelles, 1958.

5. Luke 18, 8.

6. Rom. 1, 16.

7. Heb. 13, 14.

8. Ephes. 5, 8-14.

9. *See* the official documents for the centenary of the Curé of Ars, among others, John XXIII, Encyclical *Sacerdotii Nostri Primordia* in *A.A.S.* 59

(1959), p. 545-79, *D.C.* 56 (1959), 1025-1045.—C. M. Himmer, *Lettre Pastorale,* January 8, 1959 (*Coll. Epist. Past.* 6, 1).

10. Luke 12, 49.

11. *Pontificale Romanum.*

Chapter II
Apostolic Work of Pastors

1. IN THE SERVICE OF CHRIST, OFFERING SACRIFICE IN THE MIDST OF HIS PEOPLE

1. Pius XII, *Mediator Dei,* n. 18 in *A.A.S.* 39 (1947), p. 526-27.

2. Luke 22, 19.

3. Mal. 1, 11.

4. Mark 10, 42-45.

5. Pius XII, *Mediator Dei,* n. 105-110, in *A.A.S.* 39 (1947), p. 560-62.

6. Pius XII, *Mediator Dei,* n. 98, in *A.A.S.* 39 (1947), p. 558.

7. Pius XII, *Mediator Dei,* n. 92, in *A.A.S.* 39 (1947), p. 556.

8. Canon 682. Cf. Pius XII, *Corporis Christi Mystici,* in *A.A.S.* 35 (1943), p. 193-248.

9. 1 Cor. 4, 1-2.

10. Pius XII, *Corporis Christi Mystici, loc. cit.,* p. 201-02.

11. 1 Cor. 3, 7.

2. IN THE SERVICE OF CHRIST, TEACHING IN THE MIDST OF HIS PEOPLE

1. John 7, 16.

2. Gal. 1, 6-8.

3. John 14, 15-17.

4. Vincent of Lérins, *Commonitorium*, 22 in *RJ*. (Rouet de Journel) 2173.

5. *See* also Cardinal B. S. Alfrink on the occasion of the presentation of the new translation of the New Testament prepared by the "St. Willibrordusstichting" (February 12, 1961) in *Katholiek Archief* 16 (1961), col. 169-174.

6. Vincent of Lérins, *Commonitorium*, 2, in *RJ*. 2168.

7. Matt. 28, 20.

8. Cardinal D. Tardini, Press conference to the representatives of the world press on the Ecumenical Council (October 30, 1959), in *D.C.* 56 (1959), col. 1489-1495.

9. St. Ambrose in *R.J.* 1261.

10. G. Philips, *Le rôle du laïcat dans l'Eglise*, Tournai-Paris, 1954.

11. 2 Cor. 11, 28.

12. Luke 10, 16.

13. 2 Cor. 5, 19-20.

3. IN THE SERVICE OF CHRIST, RULING IN THE MIDST OF HIS PEOPLE

(a) *The Christian before the World*

1. *See* the Allocution of Pius XII at the second World Congress of the Lay Apostolate: "Quite apart from the small number of priests, the relations of the Church with the world demand the mediation of

lay apostles. Essentially, the 'consecratio mundi' is the work of the laymen themselves, of those who are intimately involved in economic and social life, and who take part in government and legislation. By the same token, Catholic cells among factory workers and among all laboring classes for the purpose of bringing back to the Church those who are separated from it, can only be established by the workers themselves" (*Six ans se sont écoulés*, in *A.A.S.* 49 [1957], p. 92, *D.C.* 54 [1957], col. 1417).

2. Pius XII, Allocution *Six ans se sont écoulés*, in *A.A.S.* 49 (1957), p. 92, *D.C.* (1957), col. 1418.

3. John XXIII, Christmas Radio Message 1960 in *A.A.S.* 53 (1961), p. 5-15, *D.C.* 58 (1961), col. 70-71.

4. John 15, 19.

(b) *The Lay Apostolate*

1. Luke 22, 32.

2. Matt. 28, 18-20.

3. *See* the letter of Pius XII (March 21, 1949) to Canon Cardijn on the 25th anniversary of the foundation of the JOC: "There is hope for the solution of the crushing problems that exist in the world of labor, if in the factories and workshops, there are present a number of active pioneers who are fully aware of their twofold vocation as Christians and working men, who are resolutely determined to take on their responsibilities in full, and to continue their efforts without rest of any kind until they have changed their surroundings in accordance with the requirements of the gospel" (*A.A.S.* 41 [1949], p. 325, *D.C.* 46 [1949], col. 520).

4. 1 Cor. 10, 31.

5. *See* the several Allocutions of Pius XII and John XXIII on international organizations; especially the Allocution of Pius XII (July 23, 1952) at the Congress on a Catholic's duty in international life (*Vi diamo volontieri*): "Catholics most of all are extraordinarily qualified to collaborate in the creation of that kind of atmosphere without which no action on the international plane can be stable or develop successfully. This is an atmosphere of mutual understanding whose basic characteristics are the following: mutual respect; loyalty to one another, with recognition of the same rights due to others as one claims for oneself; an attitude that sees in the children of other nations our own brothers and sisters. Catholics of the whole world should really always live in such an atmosphere" (*A.A.S.* 44 [1952], p. 626-27, *D.C.* 49 [1952], col. 1033-1034).

Conclusion

One Priest: Christ Jesus

1. 1 Tim. 4, 14.

2. Pius XII, Apostolc Constitution *Sacramentum Ordinis* in *A.A.S.* 40 (1948), p. 5-7, *D.C.* 45 (1948), col. 515-520.

3. St. Thomas *III*, q. 72, art. 5.

4. Rom. 12, 6.

5. Cardinal E. C. Suhard, *Le prêtre dans la cité*, in *D.C.* 46 (1949), col. 586, 588.

6. Apoc. 5, 9-10.